CREATING
Keepsakes
CRAPBOOK MAGAZINE

hello

ENCYCLOPEDIA *of*
Scrapbooking

CREATE

playful

**The most
complete guide
to scrapbooking
ever published**

A LEISURE ARTS PUBLICATION

THE Encyclopedia
of Scrapbooking

We have made every effort to ensure that these instructions are accurate and complete. We cannot, however, be responsible for human error, typographical mistakes, or variations in individual work.

The designs in this book are protected by copyright, however you may use the projects as inspiration for your personal use. This right is surpassed when the projects are made by employees or sold commercially.

Library of Congress Control Number: 2004117291
White, Tracy
Creating Keepsakes' *Encyclopedia of Scrapbooking*
"A Leisure Arts Publication"

Softcover ISBN 1-57486-498-X
Hardcover ISBN 1-57486-499-8

EDITOR-IN-CHIEF Tracy White

SPECIAL PROJECTS EDITOR Leslie Miller

MANAGING EDITOR Marianne Madsen

EDITOR-AT-LARGE Jana Lillie

SENIOR WRITERS Rachel Thomae, Denise Pauley

SENIOR EDITORS Vanessa Hoy, Lanna Carter

ASSOCIATE WRITER Lori Fairbanks

ASSISTANT EDITORS Britney Mellen, Brittany Beattie, Heather Jones

COPY EDITOR Kim Sandoval

EDITORIAL ASSISTANTS Joannie McBride, Fred Brewer, Gail Robinson

ART DIRECTOR Brian Tippetts

ASSOCIATE ART DIRECTOR Erin Bayless

DESIGNER Celeste Rockwood-Jones

PUBLISHER Tony Golden

FOUNDING EDITOR Lisa Bearnson

VICE PRESIDENT, GROUP PUBLISHER David O'Neil

SVP, GROUP PUBLISHING DIRECTOR Scott Wagner

VP, CFO Henry Donahue

PRIMEDIA, Inc.

CHAIRMAN Dean Nelson

PRESIDENT AND CEO Kelly Conlin

VICE-CHAIRMAN Beverly C. Chell

LEISURE ARTS, INC.

VICE PRESIDENT AND EDITOR-IN-CHIEF Sandra Graham Case
EXECUTIVE DIRECTOR OF PUBLICATIONS Cheryl Nodine Gunnells
SENIOR PUBLICATIONS DIRECTOR Susan White Sullivan
SPECIAL PROJECTS DIRECTOR Susan Frantz Wiles
DIRECTOR OF RETAIL MARKETING Stephen Wilson
DIRECTOR OF DESIGNER RELATIONS Debra Nettles
SENIOR ART OPERATIONS DIRECTOR Jeff Curtis
ART IMAGING DIRECTOR Mark Hawkins
PUBLISHING SYSTEMS ADMINISTRATOR Becky Riddle
PUBLISHING SYSTEMS ASSISTANTS Clint Hanson and John Rose
PUBLISHING SYSTEMS INTERNS Shannon Connell and Josh Hyatt

CHIEF OPERATING OFFICER Tom Siebenmorgen
DIRECTOR OF CORPORATE PLANNING AND DEVELOPMENT Laticia Mull Dittrich
VICE PRESIDENT, SALES AND MARKETING Pam Stebbins
DIRECTOR OF SALES AND SERVICES Margaret Reinold
VICE PRESIDENT, OPERATIONS Jim Dittrich
COMPTROLLER, OPERATIONS Rob Thieme
RETAIL CUSTOMER SERVICE MANAGER Stan Raynor
PRINT PRODUCTION MANAGER Fred F. Pruss

table of contents

SCRAPBOOKING FUNDAMENTALS

Discover—or brush up on—the foundations of scrapbooking with this in-depth look at the history of the hobby, the tools of the trade and some page creation basics. Fueled with a little knowledge, you'll soon be on the road to recording your own history.

PAGE CREATION BASICS

BEGINNING EMBELLISHING

With a handful of attachment and accent techniques, layouts can quickly go from simple to sensational. Discover how easy it is to take your pages to new heights with the following:

INTERMEDIATE EMBELLISHING— ADD FURTHER INTEREST

Expand your options by mastering some straightforward techniques that can add complex texture, dimension and color to your layouts. Gain a lot of look for a little effort with the subsequent ideas:

ADVANCED EMBELLISHING— EXPLORE ARTISTIC EFFECTS

Flex your creative muscle with a few advanced, artistic techniques. Roll up your sleeves and get ready to brush, melt, press and roll the most imaginative accents yet. Experiment with the following:

MORE USES FOR SCRAPBOOK SUPPLIES

APPENDIX

Creating memorable layouts requires more than just well-crafted designs and embellishments. Study these primers on the following subjects to help you in other aspects of the page-creation process:

ADDITIONAL INFORMATION

As the editor-in-chief of *Creating Keepsakes* scrapbook magazine, I have the opportunity to share my passion with a worldwide audience. Each month, *Creating Keepsakes* provides readers with timeless scrapbook basics, the latest scrapbook industry trends, and cutting-edge scrapbook techniques. From basic scrapbook page design to advanced artistic techniques, *Creating Keepsakes* reaches every level and style of scrapbooker.

I want to share something with you—something that I'm passionate about. Of course, that something is scrapbooking. I completed my first scrapbook while I was in high school and haven't looked back. Whether you're just starting out in this fantastic hobby or you're a seasoned scrapbooker, you'll discover that scrapbooking is a fabulous way to ensure that the memories you are creating today are remembered well beyond tomorrow.

Inside the *Encyclopedia of Scrapbooking*, you'll find scrapbook page ideas, clear and concise explanations of scrapbooking basics, and easy-to-follow instructions on the most popular scrapbook techniques. In addition, the book features a glossary where you can reference commonly used scrapbooking terms, articles about common scrapbooking methods and a source guide that can help you find the products mentioned in the book.

With your memories, your photos and the tips and techniques you'll find in this book, you'll be creating a keepsake that you'll be able to share with generations to come.

Enjoy,

Tracy White

Editor-in-Chief

Creating Keepsakes scrapbook magazine

introduction

When I walked to my car this morning, I saw a shiny circle glinting in the parking lot, and I almost picked it up. No, it wasn't a penny. It was a silver-and-green bottle cap that had been flattened under the wheels of someone's car. "Hmmm," I thought to myself, "that could be a great accent on a scrapbook page!"

I didn't pick up that bottle cap, but I did think of *Creating Keepsakes* contributing editor Faye Morrow Bell and the way that she often embellishes her layouts with found objects, like postage stamps, luggage tags, glossy magazine pages, receipts and more. And I thought about scrapbook artist Kelly Anderson who defines her scrapbooking style as "eclectic" and who says, "I use real-world ephemera on my pages because I feel that it adds so much interest and authenticity to my pages."

As I drove to work, I started thinking about collecting "scraps" and including them on scrapbook pages as visual elements. And I started to wonder about the phrase "scrapbook" and how the definition has evolved and changed throughout history. My questions led me to research the history of scrapbooking, where I learned that people have been collecting scraps and saving them in albums for more than 150 years.

Today, scrapbooking is the fastest growing hobby in the United States. According to *The 2004 National Survey of Scrapbooking in America,* nearly a quarter of U.S. households report one or more people participating in this hobby. In the nineteenth century, middle-class Americans were captivated by "scrapbook mania" as well. How has scrapbooking changed? How has it stayed the same?

MAGAZINE QUEEN: by Kelly Anderson
Supplies *Carstock:* Memory Lane; *Alphabet stickers:* me & my BIG ideas; *Wire coil:* 7gypsies; *Pen:* Zig Millennium, EK Success; *Other:* Magazine ephemera.

The history of "scraps"

In 1980, modern scrapbooking (using acid-free and archival materials) became popular when Marielen Christensen shared 50 volumes of her family memory books at the World Conference on Records in Utah. The albums generated so much interest that the Christensen family went on to open the first dedicated retail stamping store, Keeping Memories Alive. But how did scrapbooking get started more than 150 years ago? Read on to find out!

Collectible Stickers from The John Grossman Collection, Violette Collectible Stickers, *www.violettestickers.com*

Scrapbooking became popular after the publication of a book called *Manuscript Gleanings and Literary Scrap Book* by John Poole in 1826. This book was a bound collection of printed poems and engravings. Poole also included advice on how to collect and arrange scraps.

Scraps were printed pieces of paper, often covered with ornate designs. Stickers reminiscent of nineteenth century scraps can still be purchased in scrapbooking stores and at websites such as Violette Stickers, *www.violettestickers.com*.

The first scrapbooks were created for the display of mementoes such as pressed flowers, paper cuts, silhouettes, feathers, puzzles, poems and other bits of ephemera.

"Scrap mania" became a major feature of middle-class nineteenth century life, and publishers of scraps, scrapbooks and albums quickly responded by producing a variety of products that could be cut and pasted in albums.

The scrap collector viewed almost any material as "scrap worthy" and included a variety of elements in her scrapbook, including newspaper clippings, advertisements, engraved pictures and bits of verse.

INDOOR ADVENTURE: by Jamie Waters
Supplies *Patterned paper and metal numbers:* Scrapworks; *Chipboard letters and rub-ons:* Li'l Davis Designs; *Pen:* Pigment Pro, American Crafts.

why scrapbook?

Today's scrapbookers strive to create albums that capture a special memory of a person, place or event. Scrapbookers enjoy the challenge of creating attractive pages that tell a story. Many scrapbookers also enjoy the social act of scrapbooking and attend "crop" parties or workshops at private homes, scrapbook stores and conventions where they can create page layouts and enjoy the company of family and friends.

Scrapbooking was enjoyed for similar reasons in the nineteenth century.

The "drawing room" scrapbook was the center of social exchange and discussion in the mid-1800s. Scrapbooks were used to share thoughts and feelings and became a place to record family stories and special memories. Scrapbooks were considered cherished books that were kept in families for many years.

Scrapbooking began to decline in popularity in the early 1900s due to economic restrictions following World War I. The recession that followed forced many scrapbook-related companies out of business.

You looked so big to me on this day as I sat outside taking pictures of you. I am amazed at how fast the four years you have been in our life have gone! It seems just like yesterday sometimes that you were a little baby in my arms so dependent on me. Now you are a 4 year old little girl who is very independent and love to do things on your own. How you love to have mommy and daddy come and watch you do things and how proud you are to have us watch you. I would be lying if I said I didn't get a little sentimental on this day as I watched you riding your scooter and thinking ahead to the day your little scooter will be set aside and you will move on to the life you were created to live without your mommy and daddy. And I have to tell you I grew a little misty eyed as you looked back at me, and as if you knew what I was thinking, said "I love you Mommy!" So I want you to know that no matter how big you get and no matter where you go you will always be my little girl and we will always be here for you no matter what. And don't forget your carefree days of playing on your scooter and having mommy take your pictures and being so proud of watching you. I will always be proud of you and I look forward to the accomplishments you will achieve in this life and the great things you will do. I love you, my baby girl, don't ever forget that! And don't get upset with me when I grow a little misty eyed at how fast the years are going by and when you leave our nest to move on to the destiny you were put her to fulfill. I will always be your mommy and I know that no matter where this life takes you, you will always be my little girl!

Hip Groovy Cool Hip Groovy Cool

K

ALWAYS REMEMBER: by Heather Preckel
Supplies *Patterned and textured papers:* Chatterbox; *Buttons:* Junkitz; *Nails and molding:* Chatterbox; *Ribbon:* C.M. Offray & Son; *Stencils:* Avery; *Computer font:* CBX Wednesday, Journaling Font CD, Chatterbox; *Other:* Charm.

K: by Heather Preckel
Supplies *Textured cardstock:* Bazzill Basics Paper; *Tag:* Making Memories; *Ribbon:* Textured Trios, Michaels; *Stamping ink:* Ranger Industries; *Computer font:* CK Evolution, "Fresh Fonts" CD, *Creating Keepsakes.*

Scrapbook supplies

There are hundreds of different scrapbook albums on the market today, with the most popular sizes being 6 x 6, 12 x 12, and 8.5 x 11. Many of today's scrapbookers protect their layouts with archival sheet protectors.

Here are a few fun facts about the first scrapbook albums.

Albums

During the mid 1800s, companies such as London-based W&H Rock began producing leather albums that contained printed pages devoted to various themes. Albums included preprinted pages that were heavily embellished with images of flowers and birds.

In 1857, "carte-de-viste" albums, which contained pockets for the insertion of photographs, became popular in the United States.

Some early albums included several different weights of paper. For example, an album might include pages for displaying photographs as well as pages for doing pencil drawings and watercolor paintings.

In 1872, Mark Twain (author of books such as *Tom Sawyer* and *Huckleberry Finn)* invented a product called *Mark Twain's Adhesive Scrapbook* that included prepasted pages. This album was one of Twain's most popular books, generating the author over $50,000 in sales.

Printed Paper

Printed papers are available today in a variety of colors, patterns, materials and sizes. Papers made specifically for scrapbooking are acid-free, lignin-free and archival quality.

Did you know that today's patterned papers have a history that goes back hundreds of years?

Printed patterned paper, produced by wood or metal block, lithography or stenciling were first produced in Holland and Germany in the eighteenth century.

These papers were referred to as "Dutch Gilt" or "Dutch Flowered Papers" and featured small prints, prints inspired by damask and brocade and a liberal use of the color gold.

Although these prints were meant for lining cupboards and drawers and wrapping gifts, scrap collectors used them in their scrapbooks.

Printed pieces of stationery and embellished writing papers were also often included as decorative elements in scrapbooks.

In the 1870s, companies began producing embossed papers that consumers could use in their scrapbooks.

Embellishments

Today's scrapbookers use metal accents, rubber stamps, ink, paint, stickers, ribbon, buttons and more to embellish their pages.

In the past, scrapbookers embellished their albums with the following items.

In the nineteenth century, scrapbookers decorated their albums by cutting and pasting colorful pieces of scrap into their books.

Another popular embellishment? The Prang Company printed "album cards" that were packaged in a set of ten. The cards featured pictures of birds, flowers, landscapes and friendship verses and were specifically designed for album use.

Almost every nineteenth century scrapbook includes calling cards, elaborately decorated cards left by visitors at a host's home.

Scrapbooking essentials

Journaling

Today's scrapbookers are encouraged to write the stories behind their photographs. Stories are often written in the first person. Many scrapbookers use their computers to create journaling in a variety of fonts and then print and attach their journaling to their completed layout.

Journaling in the early days of scrapbooking followed these trends:

■ Early scrapbooks were a place to record personal thoughts and sentimental endearments in one's personal handwriting.

■ Endearments such as "Forget Me Not," "True to Thee" and "A Souvenir of Friendship" were popular quotes that were cut from scrap and pasted into albums.

■ Nineteenth century scrapbookers enjoyed including poems and song lyrics in their albums.

■ Scrapbooks were often used as a place to keep personal notes, calling cards and love letters.

■ In the nineteenth century, flourished handwriting (calligraphy with fancy sweeping lines, curves and spirals) became popular in the United States and was often used to create fancy hand lettered logos and titles for letterheads and other purposes.

Photography

Today's scrapbookers have a wide variety of photography options, including digital and disposable cameras. Scrapbookers use digital technology to edit their photographs (to remove red-eye, to change a photograph from color to black-and-white, to enlarge a photograph, to erase a scratch from an old photograph and so on). Photographs can be printed to almost any size on a range of mediums that includes glossy photo paper and art canvas. Today's scrapbookers can print their own photographs at home, using photo printers equipped with archival quality inks.

In the past, photographers were limited to the following options:

■ Professional photographers began offering their services to people who lived in small towns in the 1850s. These photographs were known as daguerreotypes.

■ Photography became popular among amateur photographers after George Eastman invented the Kodak camera in the 1880s.

■ Early photographs were developed by chemists and were returned in a decorated envelope, called a film wallet.

■ The first mass marketed camera, the Baby Brownie, appeared in 1900.

Scrapbook Idea Publications

Lisa Bearnson and Don Lambson founded *Creating Keepsakes* in the mid 1990s and helped create an explosion of magazines and books devoted to teaching consumers about the art of scrapbooking.

Did you know, however, that the first idea book to promote scrapbooking appeared in 1825?

In 1825, a serial called "The Scrapbook" was issued. This book included ideas on how to fill a blank book with pictures and newspaper clippings.

In 1832, *Fisher's Drawing Room Scrap Book,* an ornately published volume that encouraged the art of scrapbooking, was published. Each volume of this book was like a modern day coffee table book, ornately bound with embossed cloth and covered with elaborate gilt decorations on the front and back covers.

Fisher later put out a series of *Drawing-Room Scrap Sheets* that readers could decorate and bind into their own personal scrapbook.

One of the first editors of this publication was a woman named Letitia Elizabeth Landon.

CRUISIN' IN THE COUPE: by Lisa Damrosch
Supplies *Patterned paper:* SEI; *Bottle cap letters:* Li'l Davis Designs; *Brads:* Karen Foster Design; *Washers:* Target (plain) and Jest Charming (pinwheel); *Eyelets:* Making Memories; *Stamping ink:* Nick Bantock, Ranger Industries; *Computer font*: 2Peas Magic Forest, downloaded from *www.twopeasinabucket.com: Other*: Ribbon.

WINDING OUR WAY HOME

Although you tend to be exceptionally shy around neighbors and acquaintances, with your own family you definitely love to gab. Case in point – on this particular day, we had spent a few hours up American Fork Canyon enjoying its beauty and were headed home when you decided to take advantage of your captive audience. You babbled on about this and that from back in your car seat while your father and I smiled across at each other. Then, you must have noticed how much we were winding as we made our way down the canyon and remarked,

"Hey Dad, how come you keep making the car turn so much?"

"Well Mum, I'm just following the road."

(a slight pause for consideration)

"Dad, you can't follow the *road*, it doesn't have any feet!"

Miriam, age 3 – September 2001

WINDING OUR WAY HOME: by Kim Morgan
Supplies *Textured cardstock:* Bazzill Basics Paper; *Letter stamps:* All Night Media (large) and Hero Arts (small); *Stamping ink:* VersaMark, Tsukineko; *Embossing powder:* Ranger Industries; *Computer font:* California Fb, Microsoft Word; *Other:* Leaf brads.

Famous scrapbookers

LISA AND LEEZA: By Janet Poelsma
Supplies *Textured cardstock:* Bazzill Basics Paper; *Patterned paper:* Leeza Gibbons for Xyron; *Lettering template:* Eliza, Page Mini and Roxy Mini, QuicKutz; *Acrylic paint and charm:* Making Memories; *Ribbon:* Mrs. Grossman's (purple), Frills (green); *Letter rub-ons:* Chatterbox; *Stamping ink:* Tsukineko; *Embroidery floss:* DMC; *Computer font:* Wednesday, downloaded from the Internet; *Other:* metal sheet, lace, straight pin, mirror accent.

When we think of famous scrapbookers today, we think of people who have influenced the industry and celebrities who scrapbook (like Lisa Bearnson, founder of *Creating Keepsakes* and actress Leeza Gibbons, both featured on this layout created by reader Janet Poelsma).

■However, there were famous scrapbookers years ago. Take a look at these names!

■Queen Victoria had a scrapbook that she displayed at the royal palace.

■Thomas Jefferson was also an avid scrapbooker and he kept leather-bound books filled with news clippings, drawings, dried leaves and other memorabilia.

■Mark Twain (the popular and prolific writer Samuel Clemens) was such a devoted scrapbooker that he dedicated Sundays to keeping his scrapbooks up-to-date.

Have fun

As you can see, scrapbooking has changed throughout the years. These changes are a reflection of how our lives have changed throughout the last 150 years. Yet, through the changes, we see just how much remains the same: our memory albums are cherished documents that tell a story of who we are while preserving our memories for future generations. Scrapbooks are a celebration of our lives, an artistic expression of who we are, a place to have fun while recording the memories that make our lives unique.

RESOURCES

Books

Encyclopedia of Ephemera
By Maurice Rickards

The History of Printed Scraps
By Alistair Allen and Joan Hoverstadt

Remember When: A Nostalgic Trip Through the Consumer Era
By Robert Opie

Dictionary of American History
By James Adams

Magazines

Creating Keepsakes
www.creatingkeepsakes.com

Family Tree Magazine
www.familytreemagazine.com

Websites

Judy Creations (*www.judycreations.com*)
"A Short History of Scrapbooking"
by Brandie Valenzuela

Little Bit (*www.littlebit.com*)
"History of Scrapbooking"
by Debbie Hamman

Tulane University
www.tulane.edu/~wclib/timeline.html

have fun

carefree

happy

creative

SUMMER fun

Creative Summer Fun: by Joy Bohon
Supplies *Patterned papers:* Karen Foster Design and KI Memories; *Rub-ons, acrylic paint and ribbon:* Making Memories; *Acrylic accents:* KI Memories; *Clips:* 7gypsies; *Letter stickers:* Sticker Studio; *Dimensional adhesive:* Diamond Glaze, JudiKins.

tool 1 guide

Whatever page you'd like to produce or technique you'd like to try, there's probably a tool to help speed the process. From adhesives to accents, papers and more, these supplies can help you create everything from the simplest of pages to the most artistic technique. Consider the following materials and give some a try. A host of imaginative and ingenious designs await you.

adhesives

Double-stick tape
❶ Available in various widths, this tape provides a strong bond for all items, including heavy embellishments and textured materials.

Foam tape
❷ Dimensional double-stick tape elevates photos or accents for added dimension. Available in square and circle shapes of various sizes.

Glue dots
❸ Pressure-sensitive dots available in numerous sizes and thicknesses to provide a strong hold for everything from thin ribbon to heavy metal accents.

Glue sticks
❹ Housed in a swivel-up container, this paste can be dabbed on the backs of photos and paper goods.

Liquid glue
❺ Adhesive packaged in bottle, tube and pen formats for precision gluing.

Photo corners
❻ Triangular tabs with small "pockets" secure the corners of a photo to the page, allowing the photo to be easily removed later without damage.

Photo tabs
❼ Double-sided adhesive squares available in roll-on dispensers and boxes. Some tabs have protective backs that require manual removal. Ideal for photos and paper goods.

Pick-up square
❽ Hard rubber square that can "erase" excess dried adhesive.

Spray adhesive
❾ Aerosol spray that provides quick, even coverage. Ideal for large projects or sheer materials, where visible adhesive is undesirable.

albums

Half-pint
Accommodates pages approximately 8½" x 5½" and most often available in three-ring format.

Mini
Small album perfect for gifts or for including on larger layouts. It comes ready-made or can be custom made with tags, cardstock and other elements.

Post-bound
Album featuring two or three metal posts that hold top-loading page protectors. Many can be expanded with post extenders.

Spiral-bound
Album with pages held together by a metal or plastic coil. Requires side-loading page protectors.

Strap-hinge
Album with pages (that must be used as the layout background or covered with other paper) held together by a plastic strap. Requires side-loading page protectors.

Three-ring
Album featuring three round or "D"-shaped rings that hold top-loading page protectors. Easy to add and remove pages, but with wide gutter between facing pages.

SHEET PROTECTORS

Side-loading page protectors—*Clear or matte protectors closed along the top, bottom and outside edge that slip onto pages already bound into albums.*

Top-loading page protectors—*Clear or matte protectors sealed along the bottom and sides, allowing pages to be slipped in from the top.*

TOOLS colorants

Acrylic paint
Water-based, synthetic paint that dries quickly. Can be thinned with water, texturized, dry brushed and used to paint accents.

Spray paint
Matte or glossy aerosol paint in numerous solid and metallic hues. Also available in a variety of faux textures, such as stone, suede and webbing.

SHORT
KRYLON®
CUTS™

HOBBY/CRAFT ENAMEL PAINT
SCS-048 SAFFRON

DANGER: Extremely Flammable. Contents Under Pressure. May be harmful if Inhaled. See cautions on back panel.

3 oz. Net Weight (85 G)

Watercolors

Water-soluble pigments used for painting and shading images. Also offered in pencil format that can be set with a wet brush or blender pen.

Chalk

Powdery, featherweight medium used to shade or color images. Can be applied with an applicator, sponge, cotton ball or fingertip.

Metallic rub-ons

Creamy medium used to add metallic sheen or shading to paper elements. Can be applied with a brush, sponge or fingertip.

Pigment powder
Fine powder (often extracted from minerals) that can be combined with gum Arabic, paint, ink and other media to produce shimmery or textured finishes.

Dye
Liquid or powder colorant designed to re-color fabrics. Can be used to color wash cardstock and other materials.

Walnut ink
Used to dye, stain or color wash paper, fabric and other materials. Available in liquid, ink and crystal forms and a variety of colors.

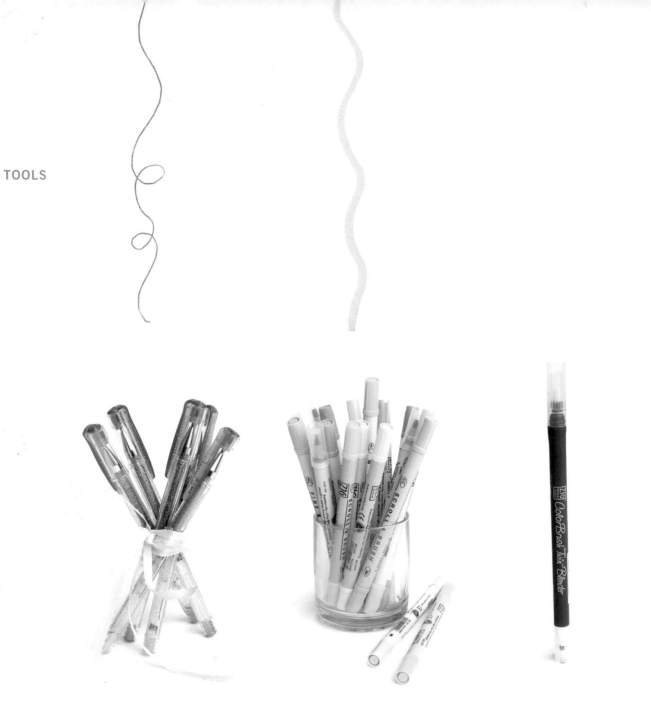

Gel pen
Ball-point pen with smooth-flowing opaque or metallic ink.

Marker
Pen used for coloring, shading and writing.

Colorless blender
Pencil or marker designed to soften, blend or seal chalked, water colored or stamped images.

APPLICATORS

Paint brushes—*Tools in a variety of widths, textures and tip shapes. Used to paint solid swatches, color washes and textures.*

Sponges—*Fibrous material used to apply a variety of colorants. Sea sponges, make-up applicators and kitchen sponges are commonly used.*

Spritzer—*Manually operated "air gun" that forces air across the tip of a marker, blowing the ink onto the paper in a concentrated spray.*

Chalk eraser—*Special white rubber eraser designed to correct chalking mistakes.*

cutters

Guillotine trimmer
Trimmer with a long, sharp blade hinged at the top that can be lifted up, then pressed down to make a straight cut.

Personal paper trimmer
Trimmer that features a safety blade designed to trim paper and photos.

Rotary trimmer
Trimmer featuring an interchangeable rotary blade. Some blade arms are connected at both ends (so paper must be slipped under for cutting). Others are hinged and can be lifted away. Rotary blades are also available in hand-held models and in a variety of decorative blade patterns.

Circle cutter
Guided tool used to cut a perfect circle. Used with a grid and cutting mat or glass plate, some units offer interchangeable attachments that cut other shapes.

Craft knife
❶ Knife featuring a straight blade for making linear cuts, often along a ruler or T-square. Some varieties feature a swivel blade to make template cutting easier.

Die cut machine
❷ Device that uses a press or rollers to push a sharp steel rule into materials to cut a precision shape.

Paper punches
❸ Tools constructed of metal and plastic that can quickly punch through materials to generate a specific shape.

Scissors
❹ Cutting tools that feature straight blades for ordinary cuts or decorative styles to produce a variety of edges.

Scoring blade (not pictured)
Blade designed to leave an indention in papers to help produce a crisp, clean fold.

Self-healing cutting mat
❺ Flexible cutting surface (ideal for use with craft knives and some circle cutters) that don't show wear, even after multiple cuts.

Shape template
❻ Templates with numerous tracks to be used with a swivel knife to produce a variety of basic shapes.

T-square
❼ Drafting tool with a long ruler and cross bar used to draw straight and parallel lines. Can also assist in making long, straight cuts.

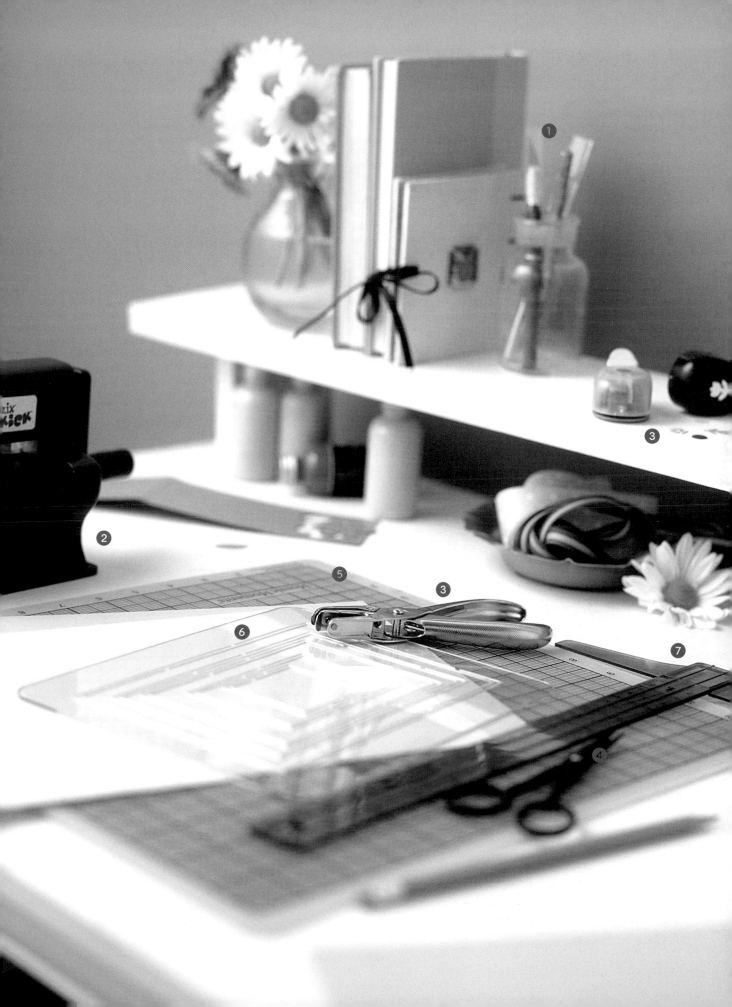

dry embossing tools

Adhesive Tech™
PORTABLE LIGHT BOX

Light box
Electric or battery-powered light source used to illuminate
a template's outline so it can be seen through cardstock.

Embossing stylus

Blunt, round tipped tool designed to press into card-stock (or other materials) to produce a dimensional image. Usually used with a shape template.

Templates

Negative portion of a cut-out shape, usually made of brass, cardboard or plastic. Templates can be traced with an embossing stylus to create raised or recessed designs.

Acrylic shapes

1 Lightweight, colorful plastic pieces cut into shapes that are plain or etched with designs, letters or words.

Alphabets

2 Offered in metal, wood, acrylic and fabric varieties, these small, dimensional shapes feature letters either printed or etched onto the surface.

Bottle caps

3 Dimensional metal pieces topped with words, patterns and motifs.

Buckles

4 Shaped closures created from etched metal or acrylic that allow ribbon and other fabrics to be threaded through.

Buttons

5 Decorated closures in various shapes, sizes, thicknesses and themes that can be adhered by stitching through holes or a shank.

Charms

6 Die cast metal pieces in a wide variety of themes. Ideal for stringing with ribbon, embroidery floss or fibers.

Jewelry findings

7 Metal jewelry parts such as hooks, clips, chains and charms.

Leather shapes

8 Shaped accents, frames or corners cut from plain, colored or embossed leather.

Metal plaques

9 Thin metal plates (often pewter colored) etched with themed designs.

Pressed flowers

10 Real flowers and leaves that have been pressed and dried.

Rocks

11 Often flat on one side for easy mounting, these pebbles are etched with designs or words.

Sea glass

12 Small chips of colorful, clear glass used in mosaics or as dimensional accents.

Shells

13 Tiny dried sand dollars, seahorses or shells.

Silk flowers

14 Lightweight faux flowers in a variety of styles. Also offered in paper formats.

Washers

15 Flat metallic circles with the center punched out. They are frequently etched with themed expressions.

Wax seals

16 Melted wax accents pressed with designs such as leaves, hearts, swirls and letters.

Woven labels

17 Fabric tags, similar to those found in clothing, with colorful themed words and expressions.

Zippers

18 Self-adhesive metal or plastic closures that can "hold" two sides of an accent together. Often adorned with charms or etched acrylic zipper pulls.

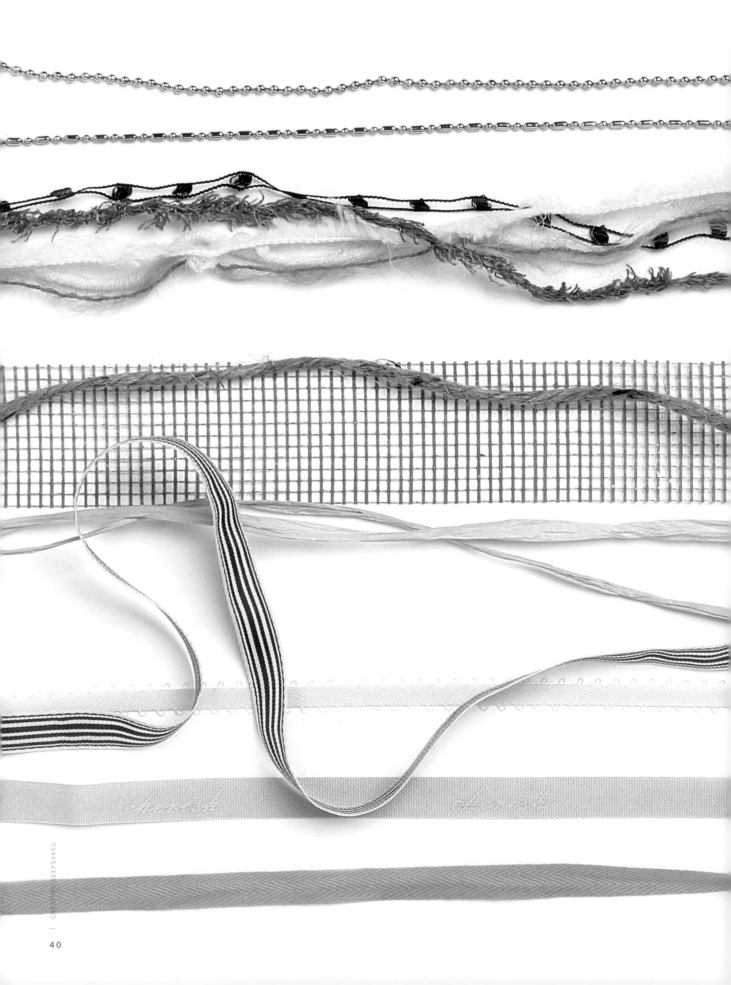

CREATIVE KEEPSAKES

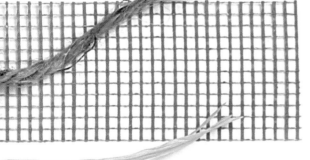

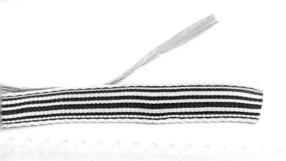

Bead chain
Lengths of lightweight ball chain used to hang accents or affix items to layouts.

Fibers
Yarn or strings available in numerous colors, textures and thicknesses.

Jute
Strong string or thin rope, often manufactured from plant fibers.

Mesh
Self-adhesive, pressure-sensitive mesh available in a variety of colors and weaves.

Raffia
Fibers (often taken from the raffia palm) used like ribbon and string.

Ribbon
Trimming that can be tied, woven, stamped or used to string accents. May be plain, printed or woven and created from materials such as silk and organza.

Twill tape
Flat cotton strips similar to ribbon. Often pre-printed with words and expressions.

Beads
Drilled, holeless, round, shaped or etched accents that add dimension and interest to accents and backgrounds.

Glitter
Lightweight, metallic flakes adhered with liquid glue or tape for a textured, sparkling finish.

Leaf flake
Featherweight metal flakes adhered with liquid glues or tape for a gilded finish.

Bottles
Miniature glass containers with metal or cork caps and loops that allow them to be strung or hung.

Compact discs
Circular discs that can be used as backgrounds for altered accents or collage designs.

Dominos
Various-sized game pieces that can be altered with inks, stamps and more for collage and page elements.

File folders
Mini versions of traditional manila folders perfect for holding journaling, memorabilia and photos. They can also be used as decorated accents.

Label holders
Metal, plastic or acrylic book plates with an open center for displaying text or pictures. Most holders feature holes on each end to accommodate fasteners.

Library pockets
Envelopes traditionally used to house checkout cards in library books. These pockets can hold photos, journaling or memorabilia.

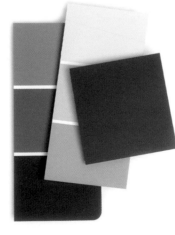

Mica
Translucent, heat-resistant tiles easily peeled into paper-thin layers for layering, pressing or heat embossing.

Microscope slides
Traditional plastic or glass slides used as accents or as part of a collage design.

Mini envelopes
Small holders or credit card sleeves created from patterned paper, cardstock, glassine or vellum.

Negative sleeves
Designed to hold film negatives, these strips have openings to showcase small photos and other accents.

Paint chips
Paper strips that display samples of household paint colors and combinations.

Quilling strips
Narrow strips of thin paper rolled on a metal tool to create coiled images.

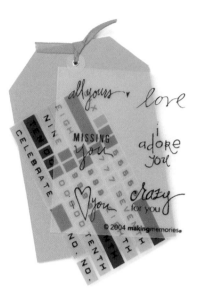

Rub-ons
Alphabet and images that can be transferred to backgrounds with a stylus or stick.

Slide mounts
Plastic or cardboard squares designed to hold slides. Can double as mini frames for small photos and embellishments.

Tags
Strips of paper that may have a hole at the top for looping string. Available in a variety of sizes and cut from cardstock, vellum and fabric.

Tiles
Shaped accents created from metal, cardboard or acrylic. They can be embellished with stamps, inks and other colorants.

Watch crystals
Plastic or glass "domes" that can serve as mini frames or small shaker windows.

Watch parts
Tiny metal coils, dials and screws.

Die cuts

Shapes cut from cardstock and other materials. Some varieties are
laser cut with intricate detail. Others are pre-printed with colorful designs.

Epoxy stickers
Dimensional, resin stickers that feature letters, words or images.

Pre-made punch outs
Cardstock accents pre-printed with designs, photos or words. Some feature slightly dimensional photos or designs.

Stickers
Glossy or matte self-adhesive images, words and designs.

fasteners

Brads

❶ Metal fasteners with prongs that can be inserted through multiple materials and flared in back to secure. Available in a variety of shapes, sizes, colors and patterns.

Clips

❷ Metal or plastic clips in a plethora of shapes and colors used to keep papers together.

Conchos

❸ Metal object with several sharp prongs that are pushed through cardstock and bent flat to secure. Available in a variety of shapes, colors, sizes, designs and metals.

Eyelets

❹ Round or shaped fasteners that must be attached with a metal eyelet setter to flatten and secure.

Hinges

❺ Bendable metal flaps attached with eyelets, brads or adhesives that attach two elements together, allowing the top item to be turned.

Photo turns

❻ Small, pointed metal pieces attached with an eyelet or brad to secure photos or flat embellishments.

Twist ties

❼ Paper-coated wire strips that can be bent or twisted to hold items together. Available in numerous colors and with pre-printed sentiments.

art media

Crackle medium

1 Used with acrylic paint, this paint-like medium creates antiqued crackle finishes when dried.

Decoupage glaze

2 Adhesive used to adhere and seal layers of paper and ephemera to form a smooth surface in collage design.

Dimensional glues and glazes

3 Glossy adhesives designed to retain shape and dimension after drying. Can be used to coat accents, create freehand designs or retain stamped impressions.

Gel medium

4 Cloudy medium used to texturize, adhere, blend with paint or pigment powder or transfer images. Some varieties feature colors or inclusions such as micro beads or sand.

Gesso

5 Water-based medium, often created from a mixture of whiting and glue, used to prime surfaces (such as canvas or metal) for painting.

Gum Arabic

6 Water-soluble gum (from the acacia tree) used as a binder for pigment powders or as a solution to increase the gloss of watercolors.

Hot glue

7 Solid glue sticks melted within an electric glue gun. Adhesive can be used as an adhesive or as the base for dimensional and textural effects.

Texture paste

8 Medium in a variety of consistencies used to create textures, finishes or unique stamped images.

7

paper/backgrounds

Cardstock

Heavyweight, acid-free paper available in a plethora of colors, weights, textures and patterns.

Cork

Lightweight sheets of bark that can be cut, punched, stamped, heat embossed and more.

Fabric

Knitted fibers in a plethora of textures, colors, patterns, weights and weaves that can be used as backgrounds and as part of dimensional accents.

Metal sheets

Thin metallic panes in gold, silver or bronze that can be stamped, embossed, crimped or punched. Available in solid or mesh varieties.

Patterned paper

Acid-free paper created in a variety of colors, designs and themes used to add interest to backgrounds and accents.

Specialty paper

Handmade and fabricated papers created from natural materials for a variety of looks and textures. Types include mulberry paper, mesh-like maruyama, pulp paper with inclusions and styles with rich, dyed designs.

Transparencies

Clear (or pre-printed) acetate sheets ideal for overlays, windows and backgrounds. Many varieties are heat-resistant and can handle computer printers and heat embossing.

Vellum

Semi-translucent paper available in a variety of colors and textures for layering, stamping, dry embossing and more.

Chalk ink
Dye and pigment inks that produce soft, powdery and often opaque images.

Dye ink
Water-based ink that dries quickly.

Pigment ink
Slow-drying, fade resistant and permanent opaque ink: Ideal for heat embossing.

Solvent ink
Opaque ink that dries quickly on most surfaces, including metal, glass, plastic and fabric.

Brayer

❶ Roller used to spread ink and other media onto cardstock. Can also be used as a burnisher.

Stamp positioner

L-shaped tool that assists in placing stamped images in specific spots. Used with transparencies, tissue paper or a clear acrylic plate.

Un-mounted rubber stamps

❷ Images carved into rubber sheets that must be trimmed and mounted—permanently or temporarily— on a wood, acrylic or metal base before use.

Wood-mounted rubber stamps

❸ Images carved into a rubber sheet and adhered to a wood block.

technology

Digital camera
Camera that captures pictures as downloadable electronic images rather than on film.

Photo printer
Inkjet printers that use photo dye ink to produce high-quality images on photo-quality paper. Some printers feature ports allowing you to print directly from a digital camera's memory card.

Photo-editing software
Program used to size, manipulate, improve and save scanned photos. Can also "stitch" 12 x 12 scans together.

Scanner
Device used to read an image, digitize and transfer it into a digital file for storing, printing, manipulating or e-mailing.

Software
Computer programs available to assist in many facets of scrapbooking. Programs may include downloadable fonts for journaling and titles, clip art as accents or paper piecing patterns, and functions that help create computer-generated layouts and elements.

other tools

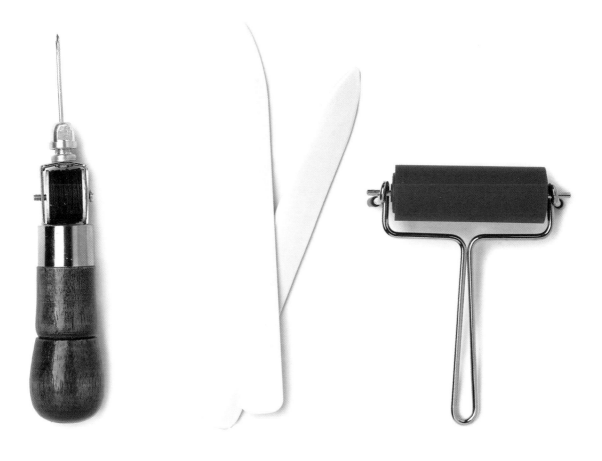

Awl
Small tool with a tapered, pointed tip used to punch holes in leather and other materials.

Bone folder
Curved tool designed to help fold, crease, score and burnish cardstock.

Burnisher
Tool used to smooth, compact or set material.

Melting pot
Electric heating device used to melt and hold art media, such as embossing enamel. Elements can be dipped into the melted liquid or poured into a mold.

Paper crimper
Tool that uses two rollers to give a corrugated texture to cardstock or metal sheets.

Paper piercer
Metal tool with a needle-sharp point used to poke small holes.

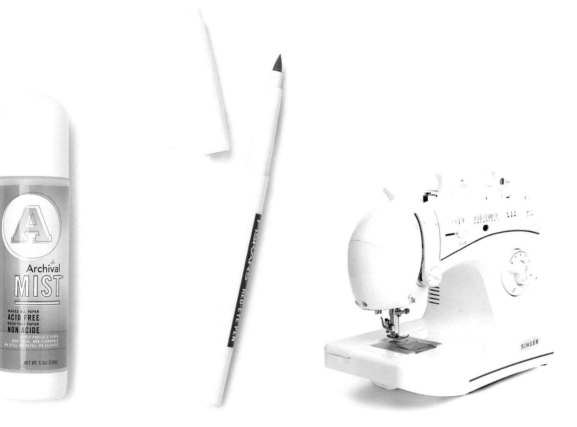

Preservation spray
Product designed to deacidify
paper products by neutralizing
the acidity.

Red-eye pen
Pen used to blot out red glare from
a subject's eyes in photos.

Sewing machine
Machine that can be used to
create decorative edges and to
sew fabric and other materials
onto backgrounds.

page creation basics

Even the most basic page requires a few tools and techniques that can ease you through the creative process. The ability to use a paper trimmer or measure a photo mat, for example, is second nature to the seasoned scrapbooker. For those just learning—or who need a refresher—here are the steps to common scrapbooking skills that will help make your next scrap session an enjoyable one.

Anatomy of a layout

Layouts can feature several "standard" elements that add to their appearance, theme, meaning and impact. When creating each page, pick and choose from the following components and design them to complement your photos and convey the story visualized in your mind's eye:

Accent

❶ Any embellishment used to adorn and decorate a page. Items can support the theme of the layout, mirror the photos or simply add dimension, texture or glitz. Anything from stickers to silk flowers to elaborately stamped designs can be used to add visual interest. (For a glimpse at some popular accents, consult the "Embellishments" section of the Tool Guide on pages 38–47.)

Border

❷ A decorative strip along the side or periphery of the layout. Borders can be created in an array of styles, comprised of a variety of materials and adorned with embellishments, photos or text. Try designing them with cardstock, patterned paper, fabric, mesh, metal, photos, tags, ephemera and more. Experiment with placement (at an angle or off the edge, for example) to add even more appeal.

Journaling

❸ The text that explains or expands upon the "story" you want the photos to convey. Journaling—which takes the form of basic names and dates, captions, lists, descriptions, quotes, lyrics or heartfelt letters— can be presented in a basic block, as an overlay, atop other elements or hidden. (For additional journaling tips and techniques, see the Appendix on pages 300–303.)

Mat

❹ Element that rests beneath a photo, often leaving an eye-catching border around the periphery. Narrow, wide, flat, dimensional, plain or elaborate, mats can draw attention to a focal-point photo, reflect the page theme or simply serve as a decorative component. Get creative and experiment with everything from plain cardstock and patterned paper to stitched fabric, a swatch of acrylic paint or a bed of ephemera.

Photo Corners

❺ The anchors that "hold" a photo, functionally or decoratively. When used as originally designed, pocketed corners are the only element affixing the photo to the page, allowing it to be removed easily at a later time. When used as embellishments, corners are created from accents such as ribbon, metal shapes, punches or cardstock strips and merely adorn a photo that's already attached to the background.

Title

❻ The words that summarize, suggest or support the page theme—anything from the event or subject's name to a thought, pun or famous slogan. A title can be placed anywhere on the layout, but is often one of the first elements to attract the viewer's eye. Text can be handwritten, computer generated, cut from templates, stamped, stenciled or created with stickers, letter tiles or other embellishments.

ERIN at 6

Watching home movies the other day, you were mesmerized by yourself at age three...chubby cheeks, pudgy arms, little voice wailing in protest during a tantrum, something about a chicken nugget.

"Baby Erin," you said as you watched, standing nearly a foot taller, tongue pushing playfully through the gap of your first lost tooth.

If you noticed the change, imagine what it's like for me. You're now longer and leaner, prone to foot stomping, huffy tantrums instead and more inclined to carry your purse with wallet, keys and makeup (like mommy!) than a chicken nugget. What will we think of this Erin when we look back at age nine? Will you still love dipping graham crackers into pudding? Watching Spongebob? Collecting Disney pins and pamphlets? Writing in your Minnie notebook? Will you still cling to my side and get angry when Ryan reaches me for a hug first? I look forward to the changes (no more tantrums, please!) and hope you know that I loved you then, love you now...and always will.

Using a paper trimmer

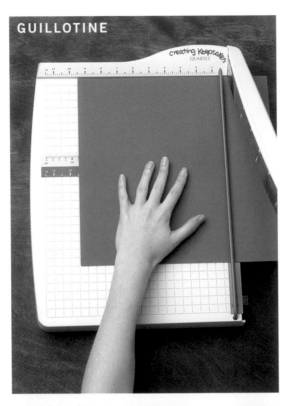

GUILLOTINE

With the proper paper trimmer, smooth and straight cuts are a breeze. Make quick work of photo cropping and paper trimming. Slice through specialty paper, mesh, thin metal sheets and more. Experiment with the following varieties to find the style that's best for you:

GUILLOTINE TRIMMER

Step 1:
■ Lift the cutting arm.

Step 2:
■ Insert the cardstock flush against the top edge of the cutter. Position your cutting mark directly below the blade. You can use the grid on the trimmer base to measure your cut.

Step 3:
■ Holding the cardstock in place with your left hand, slowly lower the cutting arm with your right hand.

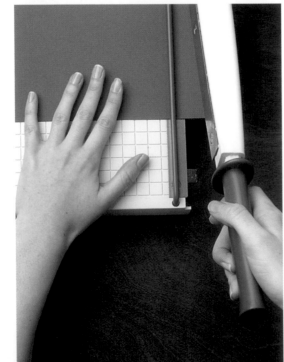

ROTARY TRIMMER

Step 1:

■ Slip the cardstock beneath the arm, flush against the top of the trimmer. (Some rotary models have cutting arms that lift out of the way.)

Step 2:

■ Holding the cardstock in place with your left hand, press the blade housing down with your palm and run it along the edge of the cutter. (Hint: If the cut edge is frayed, the blade may be dull and needs to be changed.)

VARIATIONS • • • *Several rotary trimmer manufacturers make interchangeable decorative blades to create a variety of edge styles. Rotary blades can also be used in hand-held tools (which resemble pizza cutters).*

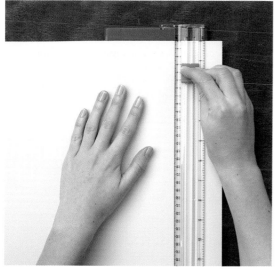

PERSONAL PAPER TRIMMER

Step 1:

■ Lift the cutting arm up and out of the way. Make sure the plastic blade housing is at the top or bottom of the trimmer.

Step 2:

■ Insert the cardstock under the arm, placing it flush against the top or bottom edge of the trimmer. Line your cutting mark up with the blade track in the base of the trimmer. You can use the grid on the base to measure your cut.

Step 3:

■ Lower the cutting arm.

Step 4:

■ Press the blade housing down with your fingertips and thumb and run it across the cardstock to cut. (Hint: If the cut edge is frayed, you need to change the blade.)

ROTARY

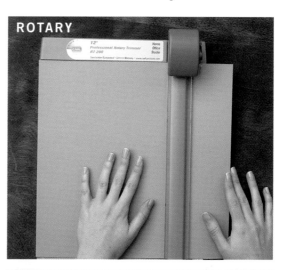

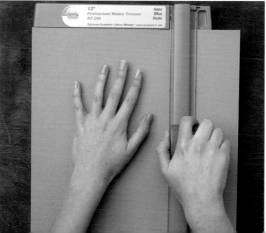

Cutting template shapes with scissors

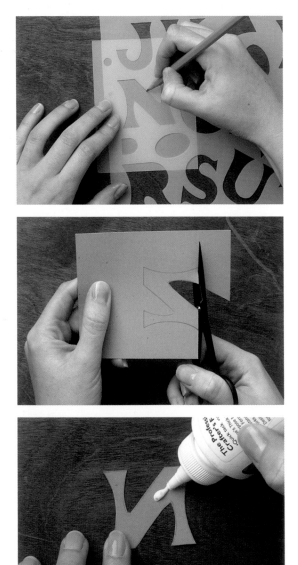

This simple trace-and-cut technique is the basis for everything from hand-cut lettering and original flourishes to paper piecing and freehand photo mats. Learn the tricks and practice regularly to create charming, homespun looks.

Step 1:

■ Place the front of the cardstock (or other paper) face down on a flat surface. (This will prevent pencil lines from showing on the finished product and eliminate the need to erase stray marks.)

Step 2:

■ Flip your lettering template or stencil over so the letters read backwards. Trace the letter onto the cardstock with a pencil.

Step 3:

■ Use sharp, pointed scissors to cut along the pencil lines. To cut smooth curves, turn the paper, not the scissors, as you round corners. (Hint: Use a hole punch to start the letter centers so you won't wrinkle the cardstock trying to poke scissors through.)

Step 4:

■ Once the letters are cut, flip them over and adhere with liquid adhesive, adhesive dots or double-stick tape. Or, add dimension with foam tape, if desired.

VARIATIONS • • • *Instead of hand cutting titles, use a pen to trace the letters' outlines and fill in with colored pencils, pens or paints. Dab an inked sponge over the template or brush over it with acrylic paint. Rather than using cardboard stencils as templates, decorate the stencils themselves with stamps, pens or paint. You can also print a title from your computer, trace, and cut around it.*

Supplies *Lettering template:* Provo Craft.

Six long months after Julia developed pericarditis and a persistent pericardial rub, she now is a picture of health. The scare she gave us seems long ago. I am so grateful to see the return of her sparkling eyes and overly enthusiastic personality. These pictures are proof. My Julia is back. My Julia is back!!!

A PICTURE OF HEALTH: by Michelle Pendleton
Supplies *Patterned paper:* Chatterbox; *Lettering template:* Chunkies, Wordsworth; *Fibers:* Greatballsoffiber.com; *Metal clip:* Club Scrap; *Metal tag:* Making Memories; *Eyelet:* Creative Impressions; *Computer fonts:* 2Peas Flea Market Block Irregular, 2Peas Falling Leaves, 2Peas Chicken Shack, downloaded from *www.twopeasinabucket.com*; CK Storybook, "The Best of Creative Lettering" Super Combo CD, *Creating Keepsakes*; CBX Wednesday, Journaling Font CD, Chatterbox; *Chalking ink:* ColorBox, Clearsnap; *Paper glaze:* Aleene's Paper Glaze, Duncan Enterprises; *Embroidery floss:* DMC; *Watermark ink:* VersaMark, Tsukineko; *Pop dots:* All Night Media; *Jump rings:* Westrim Crafts; *Stamping ink:* StazOn, Tsukineko; *Colored pencils:* Prismacolor, Sanford.

MERRY CHRISTMAS: by Jenny Jackson
Supplies *Computer fonts:* Times New Roman, Microsoft Word; Adorable, downloaded from the Internet.

having A ball

Dayna loved playing with the new BIG balls that Grandma Joan had bought for the backyard. With three 2-year-old grand-daughters, there has to be three big balls too. One afternoon Dayna spent a few minutes entertaining herself by trying to sit on the ball. It definately kept her busy! And she was having a ball! June 2004

HAVING A BALL: by Jenny Jackson
Supplies *Patterned papers:* Paper Adventures (flower) and Karen Foster Design (blue); *Letter squares:* Scrapworks; *Ribbon:* C.M. Offray & Son; *Charm:* The Card Connection; *Stamping ink:* Close To My Heart; *Computer fonts:* CK Twilight, "Fresh Fonts" CD, *Creating Keepsakes;* Times New Roman, Microsoft Word; *Other:* Stitching.

Using a red-eye pen

Say goodbye to red eye. If the subjects in your photos suffer from the flash's ghoulish red glare, simply blot it out with a marker designed for this purpose.

Step 1:
■ Test the pen tip for any dry or sharp edges that might scratch the photo.

Step 2:
■ Place the photo on a flat surface. Dab the pen gently on the red area until the glare is gone. Allow to dry completely.

Cutting with a craft knife

For precision cutting, a craft knife is the perfect solution. With a self-healing cutting mat, a consistently sharp blade and a little practice, you're sure to produce crisp, flawless cuts. As you become accustomed to this tool, you may choose it over scissors when creating title lettering, trimming cardstock or carving intricate designs.

Step 1:
■ Place the front of the cardstock (or other paper) face down on a flat surface. Trace (or print) your shape in reverse onto the back of the cardstock.

Step 2:
■ Place the cardstock on a self-healing mat. Press the tip of the knife into the cardstock and guide it toward you, holding the paper steady with your other hand. (Hint: Experiment to find the cutting style most effective for you. For example, some artists hold the knife like a pen—either perpendicular to the cardstock or at a slight angle. Others hold it in their palm with the tip of the index finger guiding the blade.)

In Chandler's opinion there are only two ways to eat watermelon First: "With my favorite watermelon spoon" (a melon baller): this is the method of choice when he is eating the 'bowl'. Second: picking it up and eating it with his mouth; this is used whenever eating any other part because he likes it cut into triangles. And when he eats watermelon like this, he eats practically the whole rind. On this day, he insisted on keeping the watermelon in a circle and eating the whole circle with the melon baller. I shouldn't have been surprised to see him pick up his entire circle of watermelon to finish off the rind, but he caught me off guard and definitely gave me a good laugh.

WATERMELON DELIGHT: by Darcee Wadduops
Supplies *Ribbon:* Making Memories; *Computer fonts:* CK Urban and CK Evolution "Fresh Fonts" CD; CK Signature, Becky Higgins' "Creative Clips and Fonts" CD, *Creating Keepsakes.*

mr personality

You are one cool, spunky and sassy kid, Joshua! At three years old, you certainly get away with much more than your brothers ever did. And you can pull it off because you just flash me any one of these cute little faces that I can't resist! You truly are Mr. Personality!

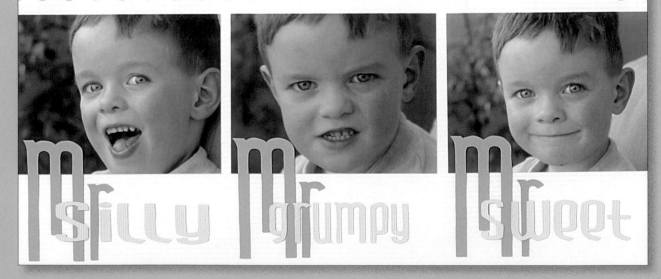

Mr silly   Mr grumpy   Mr sweet

Mr. Personality: by Stacy McFadden
Supplies *Computer fonts:* Andover, downloaded from the Internet; Times New Roman, Microsoft Word.

Measuring and cutting a photo mat

Give photos added definition or decoration with a photo mat cut from cardstock, patterned paper or other materials. Whether you'd prefer narrow, wide, tailored or torn styles, these basic steps will help you produce a multitude of mats.

Step 1:
■ Place your photo on cardstock or other matting material.

Step 2:
■ Determine how wide you want the border to be, then use a pencil and ruler to create cropping lines at each corner.

Step 3:
■ Insert the cardstock into your paper trimmer (or use a craft knife and ruler) and cut all four sides.

VARIATION • • • *For fast photo mats, adhere your photo to the cardstock first, then simply "eyeball it" using the tracks in your paper trimmer to make even cuts on all four sides.*

Cropping a photo

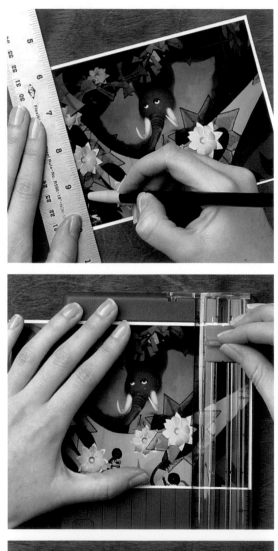

No matter how good your photography skills, there are still times when a photo has odd composition or includes unwanted elements. Master photo cropping to help reduce flaws, remove backgrounds, create artistic effects or to simply change a picture's size to suit your layout.

Step 1:

■ Determine the focal point of your photo, then decide which portions of the background detract from that image. (Hint: Consider including scenery or peripheral elements that may add historical or sentimental value years from now.)

Step 2:

■ If necessary, use a grease pencil and ruler to mark cropping lines. (You'll eventually be able to "eyeball" it and make quick cuts with your paper trimmer.)

Step 3:

■ Use a paper trimmer (or a craft knife and ruler) to make necessary cuts.

VARIATIONS • • • *To eliminate most of the background, use a large square paper punch (placed upside down so you see where you're punching) or shape cutter. To create a silhouetted image, use sharp scissors or a craft knife to cut along the outline of your subject. (If you're making drastic cuts, be sure you have a duplicate photo available in case you regret the change.)*

WYATT IS...: by Mary Larson
Supplies *Patterned paper, tags and rickrack sticker:* K & Company; *Specialty paper:* Provo Craft; *Transparency:* Narratives, Creative Imaginations; *Bookplate, buckles, photo turns and brads:* Making Memories; *Computer font:* 2Peas Crate, downloaded from *www.twopeasinabucket.com*; *Other:* Ribbon, trim and nail heads.

ROMA: by Amber Ries
Supplies *Patterned paper:* BasicGrey; *Computer fonts:* Antique Type and Applescruffs, downloaded from the Internet.

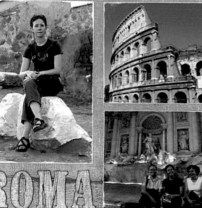

Although she complained that Rome smelled of roses and body odour, that it was hot and her feet hurt, I think Rome did Kylene good. The sunshine made her skin glow, the walking was good exercise and where else in the non-Italian world will you get delicious Gelato?

She played it cool, like it was no big deal; it was just another tiring trip with her brother-in-law who pushed her to her limits, and although they say "all roads lead to Rome", how many American women really do get the chance to travel to the city of the Holy See?

Emine and Hannah LOVE playing outside, especially if it is not blazing hot. On this July evening, the girls were having a good time just kicking the soccer ball around the yard. After the sun starts to go down, even July is bearable in the green grass! July 14, 2004

The Great Outdoors

THE GREAT OUTDOORS: by Dece Gherardini
Supplies *Textured cardstock:* Bazzill Basics Paper; *Patterned paper:* 7gypsies; *Stamping ink:* Rubber Stampede; *Rub-ons:* Making Memories; *Computer font:* CK Twilight, "Fresh Fonts" CD, *Creating Keepsakes; Other:* Ribbon and rickrack.

Adhering a photo

This is arguably the most essential, and easiest, scrapbooking skill—keeping your photos on the page! Find the adhesive that's the most effective, convenient and economical for you, then learn to apply just enough so your photos don't move.

Step 1:
■ Trim the photo to the desired size.

Step 2:
■ Flip the photo over and apply adhesive to the corners or center. (Try photo tabs, adhesive dots or double-stick tape. Xyron machines and adhesive sheets give you complete coverage if you want to adhere photos to textured materials, such as crumpled cardstock. If you choose liquid adhesives or glue sticks, use sparingly to avoid seepage and warping.)

Step 3:
■ Press your photo firmly onto the photo mat or background page.

VARIATIONS • • • *If you think you'll want to remove the photo one day, use photo corners to adhere. Simply slip one on each corner of your photo, then use the adhesive on the corners (or your own adhesive) to attach them to the page.*

Handwriting a title

Create custom page toppers by writing and designing your own title lettering. Keep it simple, add flourishes or even "cheat" by tracing over computer fonts. With a little shading from colored pencils, chalk or paints, your lettering can pull double duty as a decorative page element.

Step 1:
■ Freehand write your title in pencil, leaving space between letters if you want to add swirls or create block letters.

Step 2:
■ Add any extra lines, motifs or designs to each letter.

Step 3:
■ Trace over the letters with pen, correcting any size or shape errors. Allow the ink to dry.

Step 4:
■ Erase all pencil lines.

Step 5:
■ Fill in with colored pencils, pens, chalks or snippets of stickers and photos, if desired.

VARIATIONS • • • *Rather than handwrite, use a computer font. Simply print in the lightest shade of gray (that's still visible on your paper), then trace with a black pen.*

SWEETHEART: by Dece Gherardini

Supplies *Textured cardstock:* Bazzill Basics Paper; *Patterned papers:* SEI and Pebbles Inc.; *Ribbon:* SEI and SAS; *Circle tag:* Desert Mile Creations; *Brads:* Making Memories; *Stamping ink:* Rubber Stampede; *Pens:* Permapaque and Gelly Roll, Sakura; *Other:* Charm.

friends at first sight

Mallory & Madelynn were instant friends when they met for the first time in the summer '02. They mostly just stared & **smiled** at each other with an occasional **giggle**. Though they can't articulate their feelings just yet Kayla & I could tell that a **sweet** bond was formed between them. A **bond** not unlike the one between their mommies.

FRIENDS AT FIRST SIGHT: by Megan Jones
Supplies *Patterned paper:* Wordsworth; *Heart charm:* Prym-Dritz; *Pens:* Gelly Roll, Sakura; Zig Millennium, EK Success; *Acrylic paint:* Making Memories; *Pastels:* Prismacolor, Sanford; *Other:* Thread.

In another place and time, these sweet MEXICAN DRESSES MIGHT HAVE BEEN THE EVERYDAY WEAR FOR SARA AND EMMA. BUT, IN THE HERE AND NOW, THESE DRESSES GIVE THEM A CHANCE TO FEEL PRETTY AND SPECIAL. WHAT A WONDERFUL GIFT FROM AUNT VICKI AND ANGIE!

Señoritas Bonitas

Las Chulas

SARA, 2 YRS
EMMA, 5 MOS.
JUNE 2004

LAS CHULAS: by Linda Rodriguez
Supplies *Transparency:* Office Depot; *Flower punch:* EK Success; *Brads:* Making Memories; *Pens:* Galaxy Marker and Slick Writer, American Crafts.

beginning
embellishing

3

Ready to spice things up? Once you've mastered the basic techniques, it's surprisingly easy to give your pages added punch. A little ribbon, a few fasteners or a handful of dimensional accents can dress up your layouts and draw attention to focal point photos with finesse and flair. Whether you lean towards cute, clean or eclectic, these techniques can help you achieve your look.

Adding dimension

Take hand-cut letters, pre-made accents, photos and more to new heights with a bit of dimensional adhesive. And, because elements are elevated on flexible foam tape, they're not likely to affect facing pages.

Step 1:
■ Flip the element over. Apply foam mounting tape or dimensional adhesive dots to the back of the piece. (Hint: Don't place adhesive too close to the outside edges—it may be visible from the side.)

Step 2:
■ Press to adhere.

VARIATION • • • *Vary the height of your element(s) by applying tape to just a portion of it. Layer pieces of tape on top of each other to add even more dimension.*

Supplies *Lettering template:* ScrapPagerz.

FUN 'N' GAMES: by Ann-Marie Weis
Supplies *Patterned paper and letter rub-ons:* Chatterbox; *Title letters:* Li'l Davis Designs; *Ribbon:* Estonami Enterprises; *Date and number rub-ons:* Autumn Leaves; *Other:* Game pieces, burlap and brads.

IDEA TO NOTE: Ann-Marie wanted to add dimension to her layout, so she used children's playing cards and game pieces as page accents.

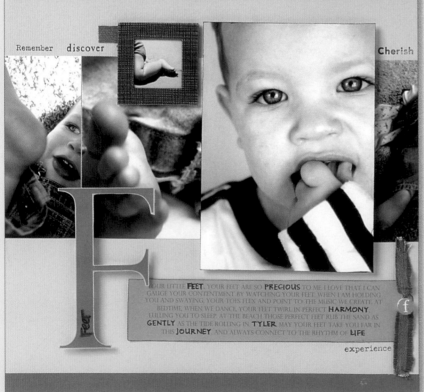

A FLOWER: by Stacy McFadden
Supplies *Patterned paper, letter cut outs and flowers:* SEI; *Bookplate:* Making Memories; *Pop dots:* Glue Dots International; *Foam tape:* 3M; *Computer font:* American Typewriter, downloaded from the Internet.

IDEA TO NOTE: To add additional dimension to her layout, Stacy used pop-up glue dots underneath her cut-out letters.

TYLER'S FEET: by Jamie Harper
Supplies *Textured cardstock:* Bazzill Basics Paper; *Large and small "F" stickers:* Chatterbox; *Rubber stamps and metal frame:* Making Memories; *Denim:* Junkitz; *Foam tape:* Scotch, 3M; *Pop dots:* Ranger Industries; *Computer font:* Times New Roman, Microsoft Word.

IDEA TO NOTE: To make the letter "F" on her layout more prominent, Jamie used foam tape underneath it to pop it up off her page.

Making a page pocket

Have too many photos to fit on your page? A handful of memorabilia you'd like to include? Some heartfelt journaling you'd rather conceal? A pocket page can contain it all! Create a functional pocket from cardstock. Or, opt for a purely decorative pouch crafted from lengths of ribbon or fiber and anchored with fasteners. Either way, "extras" will be included, out of the way and part of an attractive accent.

Step 1:
■ Trim cardstock (or a photo, postcard or other solid material) to size and decorate, if desired.

Step 2:
■ Flip the pocket over. Apply double-stick tape (or foam mounting tape for a dimensional pocket) to the bottom and sides. Press onto the background to adhere.

VARIATIONS • • • *Pockets can also be created from ribbon, mesh, fabric or anything that can be adhered along the sides to "hold" your memorabilia. Pockets can also be held in place with fasteners or hand or machine stitching.*

Supplies *Specialty paper:* Books By Hand.

2: by Candace Leonard
Supplies *Patterned Paper:* KI Memories; *Zipper:* Junkitz; *Stamps:* PSX Design; *Paint:* Delta Technical Coatings; *Ribbon:* May Arts; *Stamping ink:* Memories, Stewart Superior Corporation; *Other:* Stencil.

IDEA TO NOTE: Candace created a zipper pocket on her layout and tucked her journaling inside it.

REPORT CARD: by Ann-Marie Weis
Supplies *Patterned paper and cardstock stickers:*
Sassafras Lass; *Letter stickers:* American Crafts;
Ribbon: May Arts; *Other:* Report card.

IDEA TO NOTE: Ann-Marie created the pocket on her
layout by cutting along the wave pattern in the paper
and adhering the bottom of the pocket to her page
with Miracle Tape.

Renaissance Festival: by Kristi Barnes
Supplies *Textured cardstock:* Bazzill Basics Paper;
Large pocket: Kristi's own design; *Small pocket and
spiral clip:* Making Memories; *Square punch:* EK
Success; *Stamping ink:* Memories, Stewart Superior
Corporation; *Computer fonts:* Day Trip, downloaded
from the Internet; Times New Roman, Microsoft Word.

Customizing page protectors

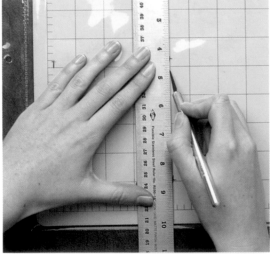

Pull-out elements, mini-books, hidden journaling and other interactive elements are perfect for adding dimension and more information onto your page. What good does it do, however, if it's completely sealed beneath a page protector? Discover how a few quick slices can give you easy access to these hands-on designs.

■ *Step 1:*

Place your layout inside a heavy-duty page protector and use a grease pencil to lightly mark the corners of your pull-out element.

■ *Step 2:*

Remove the layout, then slip a self-healing cutting mat inside the page protector. Use a craft knife and ruler to make three cuts that will create an accessible and interactive flap in the page protector.

Supplies *Patterned paper*: Creative Imaginations; *Computer fonts*: CK Newsprint, "Fresh Fonts" CD, *Creating Keepsakes*; Post It, downloaded from the Internet; *Letter stamps*: PSX Design; *Rub-ons*: Alphawear, Creative Imaginations; *Epoxy letters*: Bits and Baubles, Creative Imaginations, *Stamping ink*: StazOn, Tsukineko; *Pen*: Zig Writer, EK Success; *Tags*: DMD, Inc.; *Brad*: GoneScrappin.com.

WHAT IS A TWEEN?: by Teri Fode

Supplies *Textured cardstock:* Bazzill Basics Paper; *Patterned paper:* Rocky Mountain Scrapbook Company; *Ribbon:* C.M. Offray & Son; *Stamping ink:* PSX Design; *Foam stamps:* Making Memories; *Transparency:* OfficeMax; *Brads:* Creative Imaginations; *Flower stickers:* Jolee's Boutique, Sticko for EK Success; *Pen:* Zig Millennium, EK Success; *Computer font:* Papyrus, Microsoft Word; *Other:* Picture frame hooks.

IDEA TO NOTE: Teri tucked additional photographs and journaling inside the interactive flaps that she included on her page.

LIZ AND MIKE: by Jamie Harper
Supplies *Textured cardstock:* Bazzill Basics Paper; *Patterned paper:* SEI; *Acrylic paint:* Making Memories; *Letter stamp:* Stampers Anonymous; *Prong bases:* ACCO; *Pen:* Zig Millennium, EK Success; *Other:* Fabric, ribbon and hole punch.

IDEA TO NOTE: Jamie printed her photographs on textured cardstock to give them added texture.

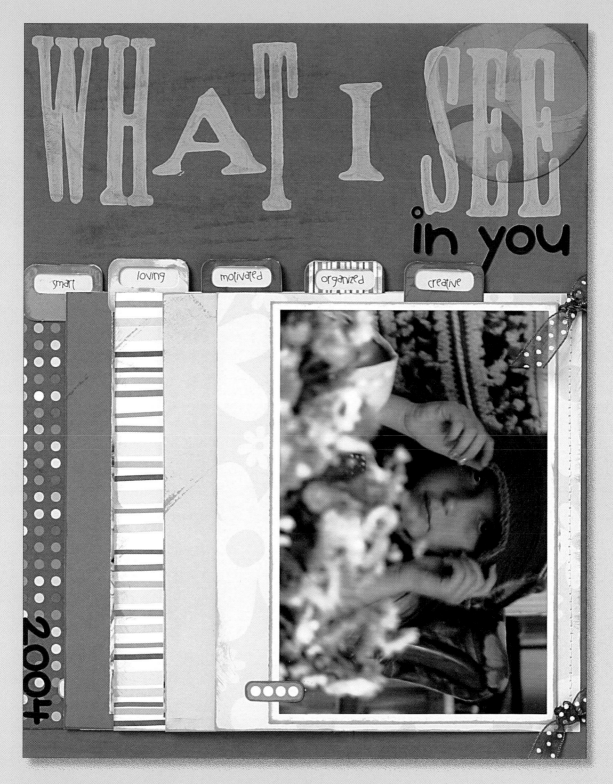

WHAT I SEE IN YOU: by Wendy Sue Anderson
Supplies *Patterned papers, tags and letter stickers:* KI Memories; *Number stickers, letter stamps and acrylic paint:* Making Memories; *Ribbon:* May Arts; *Stamping ink:* Memories, Stewart Superior Corporation; *Computer font:* 2Peas Fairy Princess, downloaded from *www.twopeasinabucket.com*; *Other:* Thread.

IDEA TO NOTE: Notice how Wendy Sue created an interactive book on her page and tabbed each section with a word that describes the pictures tucked inside the book.

Applying text rub-ons

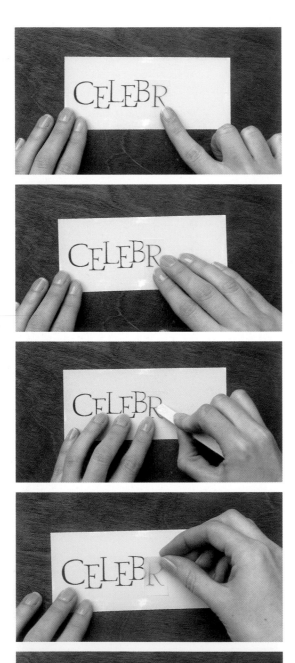

Add instant text to backgrounds and accents with rub-ons. They're more uniform than most handwriting, less messy than letter stamps and can be applied where fonts cannot. And, you can apply them to paper, glass, metal, leather, transparencies and more.

Step 1:
■ Place cardstock (or other material) on a flat surface. Remove any dust or other debris from the surface.

Step 2:
■ Remove the backing from the sheet of rub-ons and position the letter (or word) over the desired spot. (Hint: You may want to cover other portions of the cardstock to prevent stray rub-ons from adhering where they're not wanted. If they do, carefully press and lift an adhesive tab on them to remove.)

Step 3:
■ Using a bone folder, burnisher, popsicle stick, embossing stylus or your fingernail, rub over the sheet firmly until you see the rub-on peel away from its backing.

Step 4:
■ Carefully lift the sheet. If any portion has not adhered, reposition and rub again.

Step 5:
■ Place the back of the backing sheet over your finished work and burnish to be sure the rub-ons are completely flat.

Supplies *Rub-ons:* Making Memories.

pROMise me...

...yOu'll always BE you

As you sat contemplating the world outside your window this day, I stood contemplating my life with you. How our world has changed since the day we found out we were expecting you! Every day you teach us something new and bring a smile to our faces. Although our road together has barely just begun, I hope that through all the challenges that life brings your way you'll always remember to be you. Because it's you we love, in every way. April 2004.

PROMISE ME: by Joanna Bolick
Supplies *Textured cardstock*: Bazzill Basics Paper; *Patterned paper*: Rusty Pickle; *Computer fonts*: Sonoma and Italic, Mac OS X; *Rub-ons*: Li'l Davis Designs.

IDEA TO NOTE: The word "always" in this title was created by combining two different sets of rub-on alphabet letters.

THE JOY OF DISCOVERY: by Angelia Wigginton
Supplies *Textured cardstock:* Bazzill Basics Paper; *Patterned paper:* Paperfever; *Rub-ons:* K & Company; *Mini brads:* Making Memories; *Buttons:* Junkitz; *Other:* Ribbon.

FLY BY SMELLING: By Candace Leonard

Supplies *Cardstock and patterned paper:* KI Memories; *Foam stamps:* Li'l Davis Designs and Making Memories; *Paint:* Making Memories; *Rub-ons:* Making Memories, Li'l Davis Designs and KI Memories; *Buttons:* Junkitz.

Attaching clear accents

Though they bring a clean, colorful quality to layouts, clear acrylic accents can be a bit problematic. After all, nothing spoils the look of a sleek surface more than telltale adhesive showing through. With the right tools and technique, you can minimize or eliminate streaks, bubbles and blurs.

Step 1:

■ Place the clear accent face down and apply a light, even coat of spray adhesive, a single layer of double-stick tape (for smaller accents), or a clear-drying liquid adhesive. (Hint: The key is to completely cover the back of the accent so the edges of the adhesive won't show through.)

Step 2:

■ Press the accent gently onto the background. Use a toothpick or stylus to remove any excess liquid adhesive that may ooze out.

VARIATIONS • • • *If accents feature pre-drilled holes, try attaching them with brads, long eyelets, chains or ribbon.*

Supplies *Acrylic flowers:* Icicles, KI Memories.

bambino

Mom Planted this little baby rhody (it will never get very big, a small bush for a little boy) in her back garden in the summer of 2003, in memory of **Zane Alexander Sacher.**
It is blooming for the first time, just 2 months before his first *birthday*. And was just in time for Mother's Day.

Main Entry: **bam·bi·no**
Function: *noun*
Inflected Form(s): *plural -nos or* bam·bi·ni
Etymology: Italian, diminutive of *bambo* child; *plural usually bambini*

1: a child; a baby.

first blooms: May 2004

bloom

BAMBINO: by Amber Ries
Supplies *Graffiti sticker:* Art Warehouse, Creative Imaginations; *Computer fonts:* 2Peas Sunshine, downloaded from *www.twopeasinabucket.com*; Verdana, Microsoft Word.

WE WENT TO play IN THE QUIET AND tranquil LAND OF SEDONA. IN THIS PLACE, IT SEEMS THAT EVERYTHING WORKS IN harmony . DURING OUR STAY, TAYLOR AND HER FRIEND LIZZIE MADE A splash IN THE POOL AT THE RESORT AND ENJOYED THE SOUNDS OF cool OAK CREEK. IT WAS OUR TIME TO ENJOY THE SUN — TIME TO REST AND relax . THE WEEK WAS AN INVIGORATING RETREAT AND RESPITE FROM THE WORLD. IT WAS MORE WONDERFUL THAN I COULD EVER imagine .

GRASSHOPPER POINT JULY '04

GRASSHOPPER POINT: by Allison Landy
Supplies *Clear accents and rub-ons:* Heidi Grace Designs; *Clear words:* KI Memories; *Metallic rub-ons:* Craf-T Products; *Pen:* Zig Writer, EK Success; *Computer font:* Hootie, downloaded from the Internet.

When I think of our first days together, I remember ... your soft new baby skin, your teeny fingers and toes, how much you slept, your sweet baby smell, how much you didn't sleep at night, how often you nursed, how you made such funny faces, how your hair stood straight up ... how completely I fell in love with you

sweetheart

Baby

February 8, 2004

SWEETHEART: by Linda Rodriguez
Supplies *Patterned paper:* SEI; *Transparent accents:* Paper Bliss, Westrim Crafts; *Transparent letters:* K & Company; *Pen:* Gelly Roll, Sakura; *Other:* Ribbon and staples.

Attaching an eyelet

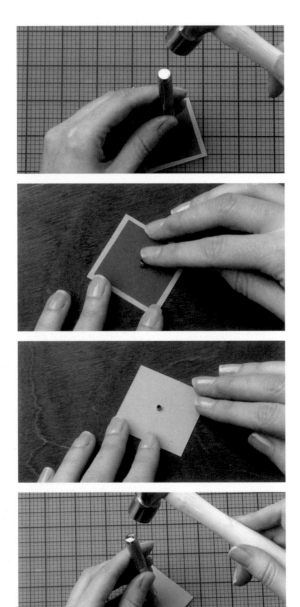

Eyelets are favorites in scrappers' tool kits and are as varied in shape and color as the uses for them. In addition to joining elements together, eyelets can be used to anchor ribbon and fiber, hang charms, and attach label holders, hinges and much, much more. It's easy to see why learning how to set them is a definite scrapbooking essential!

Step 1:
■ Use an anywhere or hand-held hole punch to create a hole that suits the eyelet size (i.e., a 1/16" hole for a micro eyelet, 1/8" for "traditional" and 1/4" for larger sizes).

Step 2:
■ Insert the eyelet into the hole from the front.

Step 3:
■ Flip the cardstock and eyelet over so the back of the paper and "raw" side of the eyelet are facing up. Place on a self-healing mat or similar surface.

Step 4:
■ Position the tip of the eyelet setter so it rests securely in the center of the eyelet at a 90-degree angle.

Step 5:
■ Use a hammer to tap the back of the setter a few times, until the back of the eyelet splits and flattens.

VARIATION • • • *Some manufacturers offer hammerless hand–held and tabletop tools or presses designed to set eyelets with minimal noise and effort. A few versions can punch a hole and set the eyelet in a single step.*

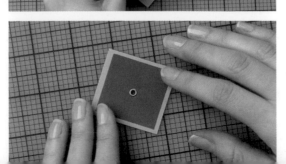

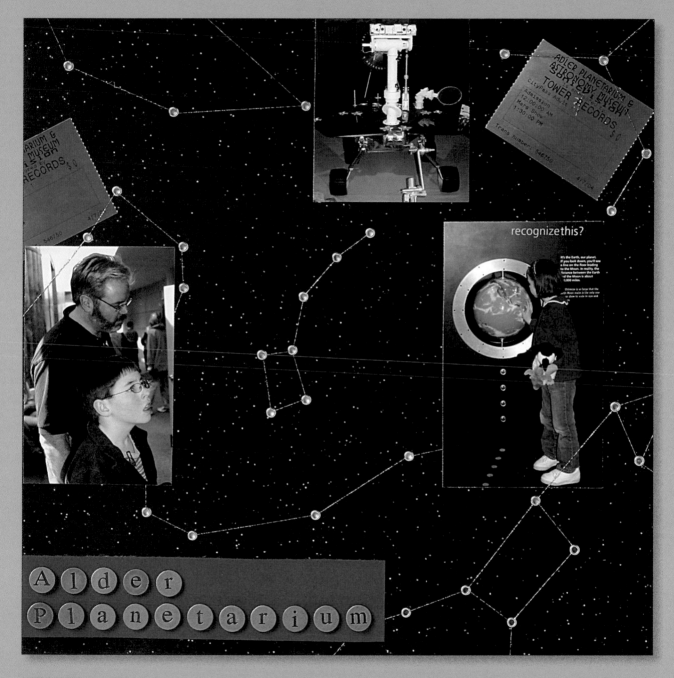

ALDER PLANETARIUM: by Sally Garrod
Supplies *Patterned paper:* Source unknown; *Eyelets and letters:* Making Memories; *Thread:* Balger.

IDEA TO NOTE: To create the constellation background on her page, Sally printed a constellation pattern from the Internet. She positioned the pattern over her cardstock and used a thick needle to poke holes in her paper. She placed a silver eyelet through each hole to represent the stars and threaded silver thread through the eyelets to represent the constellations.

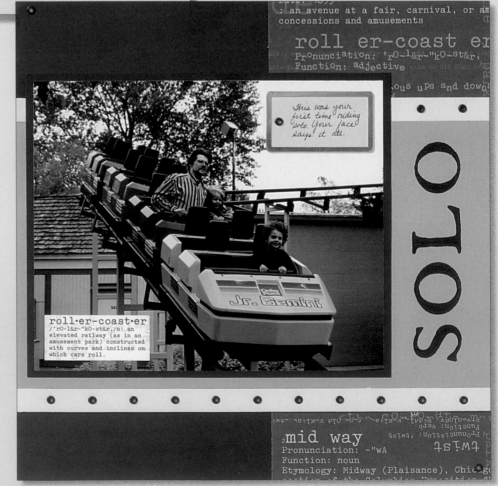

FLOWER GIRLS: by Kristi Barnes
Supplies *Tags, flowers, acrylic paint and eyelets:* Making Memories; *Stamping ink:* Memories, Stewart Superior Corporation; *Computer fonts:* Carpenter, downloaded from the Internet; CK Newsprint, "Fresh Fonts" CD, *Creating Keepsakes.*

SOLO: by Heidi Stepanova
Supplies *Patterned paper and stickers:* Karen Foster Design; *Tag, foam stamps and acrylic paint:* Making Memories; *Eyelet template:* Creek Bank Creations; *Eyelets:* Doodlebug Design; *Pen:* Zig Millennium, EK Success.

Attaching a brad

Anyone who went to elementary school probably remembers brass brads—the fasteners most often used to secure book reports and hinged craft projects. Now available in a plethora of colors, shapes and sizes, brads are the quick and easy way to affix page elements with a decorative flair.

Step 1:
■ Punch a hole (large enough to accommodate the brad's prongs without tearing the paper too much) into the cardstock. (Hint: For mini brads, a small hole punched with a paper piercer will suffice.)

Step 2:
■ Push the brad through the hole.

Step 3:
■ Flip the cardstock over and flare the brad's prongs, butterfly style, and press flat. Secure with a piece of tape, if desired.

Step 4:
■ Place cardstock face up on a flat surface and press down on the top of the brad to completely flatten.

Supplies *Brad:* Making Memories; *Specialty paper:* Black Ink; *Hemp paper:* Creative Imaginations.

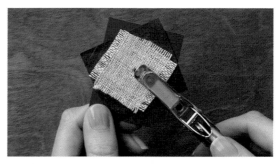

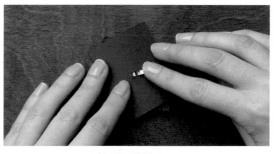

HULA LOOP

LOOP

Every girl needs a hula hoop. Or in Brenna speak..a "hula loop". I never get tired of hearing her say "hula loop"..in fact, I admit..I am guilty of encouraging the mispronunciation; it is just too stinkin cute. She can't hold the hoop parallel on both sides because her arms aren't long enough, but that hasn't stopped her from figuring out a way to get the pink ring a spinnin! Learning to shake her hips to keep the hoop from falling was a skill she mastered in no time flat. She is after all the queen of the hip shake, seems to me she was born with it!   September 2004

Hooping makes our bodies feel great. Spinning the hoop around our body and dancing with the hoop to music is fun, blissful, and creative. Hooping invokes laughter and smiles, and it improves health.   (~hooping.org)

HULA LOOP: by Miley Johnson
Supplies *Patterned paper:* KI Memories; *Letters and jump rings:* Junkitz; *Chipboard letters and acrylic paint:* Making Memories; *Ribbon:* C.M. Offray & Son; *Brads:* Déjà Views, The C-Thru Ruler Company; *Computer font:* CK Tipsy, "Fresh Fonts" CD, *Creating Keepsakes.*

August 2000

You Color my World

Callahan & Daddy

YOU COLOR MY WORLD: by Jennifer Blackham
Supplies *Textured paper and brads:* Provo Craft; *Square punches:* EK Success; *Stamping ink:* Colorbök, Clearsnap; *Computer font:* PC Kid, "The Font Factory," Provo Craft.

DESERT HIKE: by Mary Larson
Supplies *Patterned papers:* Karen Foster Design and Paper Adventures; *Hemp paper:* Artistic Scrapper, Creative Imaginations; *Brads and rub-ons:* Bradwear, Creative Imaginations; *Stencil letters and rub-ons:* Making Memories; *Computer font:* Wichita, downloaded from the Internet; *Other:* Ribbon and twill tape.

FEB 2004

desert HIKE

While on the hike, they were given a paper with several desert items and animals listed. The children were to look for them in the desert along the hike. Kurt took this very seriously and was not happy that everyone was making noise and "scaring away the animals!" Since he was determined to find everything on the list and that list contained coyotes and snakes (which, thank goodness, we didn't see!) we just pretended to see them so he could check them off. At the end of the hike, he had his list completed and was very happy.

One of the field trips Kent and Kurt's pre-school class took was to hike South Mountain. Of course it was a quick and easy "hike" - just enough for 5 year olds.

Attaching a button

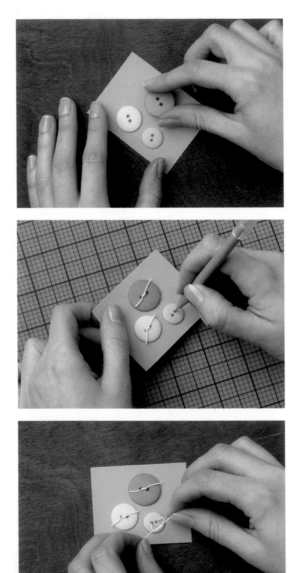

For a cute, homespun touch, add colorful buttons along photo mats borders, as the "centers" of hand-cut letters or to function as envelope and pocket closures. From traditional round shapes to geometric styles to detailed designs, you're sure to find a button or two to outfit your layout.

Step 1:
■ Tack the button in place with an adhesive dot.

Step 2:
■ Poke holes in the cardstock by inserting a paper piercer through the button holes.

Step 3:
■ Pull string, thread or fiber through the holes and knot.

VARIATIONS • • • *To save time, thread and knot the string on the button first, then simply attach the button to the cardstock with adhesive dots or glue. For buttons with shanks instead of holes, simply snip them off with wire cutters, then affix to the layout the buttons with adhesive dots.*

Supplies *Buttons:* Making Memories; *String:* Waxy Flax, Scrapworks.

RED, WHITE, BLUE AND YOU: by Heather Preckel
Supplies *Textured cardstock:* Bazzill Basics Paper; *Ribbon:* May Arts; *Buttons:* Junkitz (red) and thrift store (white); *Washers:* Lee Valley; *Labels:* Dymo; *Letter stickers:* EK Success; *Computer font:* Antique Type, downloaded from the Internet; *Other:* Charm.

bubbles

Okay, I admit it... sometimes I really don't like bubbles. Reminding you not to put your mouth on the wand, the sticky drippy mess all over your hands, clothes, and the ground, the tears when you accidentally knock the bottle over, and the pleas for me to fill it up again. Like most things, when it comes to motherhood, the things that I love more than make up for the things that I don't. I love the delight on your face when you blow a really big bubble or catch one on your wand. I love watching you chase the bubbles and try to pop them before they hit the ground. Most of all I love that you remind me to enjoy things, the little messes don't matter but the joy always does.

BUBBLES: by Bonnie Lotz
Supplies *Patterned paper and letter stickers:* KI Memories; *Buttons:* Making Memories; *Embroidery floss:* DMC; *Computer font:* Garamond, downloaded from the Internet.

OCEAN BEACH, CALIFORNIA: by Jenny Jackson
Supplies *Patterned paper:* KI Memories; *Buttons:* Making Memories and Junkitz; *Glitter and tape sheet:* Art Accents, Provo Craft; *Computer font:* CK Template, "Fresh Fonts" CD, *Creating Keepsakes.*

IDEA TO NOTE: To create the button "wave" accent on the bottom of her page, Jenny drew a pattern onto an adhesive tape sheet. She attached the buttons to the adhesive in a random pattern and then sprinkled glitter over the buttons to cover any exposed adhesive.

Attaching a concho

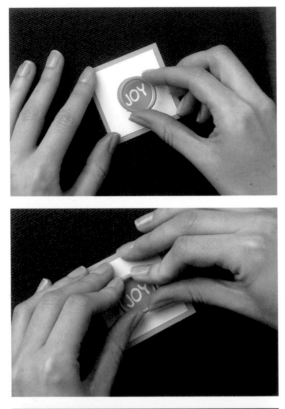

Whether you refer to them as "studs," "nailheads" or "conchos," the teeth of these metal fasteners can grab onto paper, fabric, metal and more, allowing them to connect, adhere and adorn multiple elements.

Step 1:
■ Place the cardstock over a flexible surface (such as a push pad or computer mouse pad) and position the concho as desired. (Hint: If you're using conchos to frame an accent, adhere the accent to the background first to keep it from shifting.)

Step 2:
■ Push the concho straight down until it punches completely through the cardstock.

Step 3:
■ Flip the cardstock over and use a popsicle stick or bone folder to bend each prong toward the center.

VARIATIONS • • • *Conchos can also double as frames for tiny photos and embellishments. They can also be used as faux typewriter keys when mounted over a letter stamp or sticker, filled with dimensional glaze and allowed to dry.*

Supplies *Concho and punch out: Scrapworks.*

Michaela was delighted with all the shells she found in the water at Gulf Shores. She brought me all shapes and sizes. Most were broken, but she didn't mind that one bit. They were still beautiful to her.   July, 2004

IMAGINE, SPLASH, PLAY: by Angelia Wigginton
Supplies *Patterned paper:* Paperfever; *Conchos and word circles:* Scrapworks; *Mini brads:* K & Company; *Computer font:* 2Peas Plain Jane, downloaded from *www.twopeasinabucket.com*.

3 PETS: by Mary Larson
Supplies *Patterned paper:* Karen Foster Design; *Hemp paper:* Artistic Scrapper, Creative Imaginations; *Conchos:* Scrapworks; *Transparency strip:* Art Warehouse, Creative Imaginations; *Small letters and numbers:* Bradwear, Creative Imaginations; *Letter stamps, acrylic paint, ribbon and mailbox letters:* Making Memories; *Computer font:* CK Constitution, "Fresh Fonts" CD, *Creating Keepsakes.*

30 minutes in a deprivation tank. It's on my birthday and Christmas wish lists every single year. Alas, no one has taken my request seriously. They just don't get it. I truly value silence. I don't experience it very often, so it's like a delicacy for me. From the time my 3 children's 6 little eyes pop open in the morning, until the time they finally (and blissfully) close again at night, I am surrounded, besieged, and overwhelmed by noise. Be it tantrums or shrieks of laughter, imaginary sword fights or the clack, clack, clack of toy car wheels echoing across the tiled kitchen floor, noise is everywhere and it's constant. My girlfriend, Stephanie, calls this "The House of Noise". Doors slam. Cartoons blare. Electronic, educational gizmos bleep and sing. The volume knob for my kids' voices was cranked to max and then broken off, evidently, because they don't know anything but full tilt. A reminder to "use your inside voice," usually receives "OK, MOM!!!" shouted as a response. *Sigh.* I'm sure there will come a day when the kids are grown and my house will seem so empty and quiet, and I will probably miss the chaos. Someday. But now there are days when I honestly feel I could jump out of my skin if the decibels don't decrease. It's those days when I steal away to my bedroom and close the door for 10 minutes to chant some "Ohms" in a desperate attempt for some peace. My brief zen state is usually interrupted, however, by "Mommmmmmy so-and-so did such-and-such!", and I must again forge into the din. Am I alone in my deafening madness? The only Mommy to suffer this way? I couldn't be. Speak up, ladies! Can I get an "Amen"? Oh, forget it. I probably couldn't hear you, anyway. *written sept, 04*

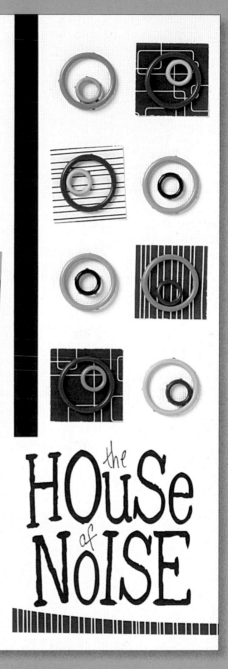

the
HOUSE
of
NOISE

THE HOUSE OF NOISE: by Gillian Nelson
Supplies *Textured cardstock:* Bazzill Basics Paper; *Patterned paper and accents:* KI Memories; *Circle accents:* Scrapworks; *Pen:* Slickwriter, American Crafts; *Computer font:* 2Peas Frazzled, downloaded from *www.twopeasinabucket.com*.

Attaching hinges

From the hardware store to scrapbook store shelves, hinges have come a long way; and it's easy to see why. Hinges are perfect for connecting and attaching items, often allowing them to conceal additional photos, journaling or other design elements. If you'd like to experiment with these cool fasteners, just grab your tool kit—your scrapbooking tool kit, of course!

Step 1:
■ Using a brad or eyelet, attach the hinge to the top photo or element.

Step 2:
■ Place the element where you'd like it to rest and attach the other half of the hinge with adhesive dots or metal glue. (Hint: You can attach the bottom half with a fastener, but it may prevent the flap from lying flat if it's too dimensional.)

VARIATIONS • • • *Hinges can also be attached "open" with brads or eyelets, allowing both halves of the hinge to be visible. They can also be adhered "closed," with the hinge glued to the back of the top element so only the narrow edge of the hinge is exposed.*

Supplies *Hinge:* Making Memories; *Rubber stamps:* Rubber Stampede ("Celebrate"), Making Memories (flourish) and Posh Impressions ("Happy Birthday"); *Stamping ink:* StazOn, Tsukineko; Marvy Matchables, Marvy Uchida.

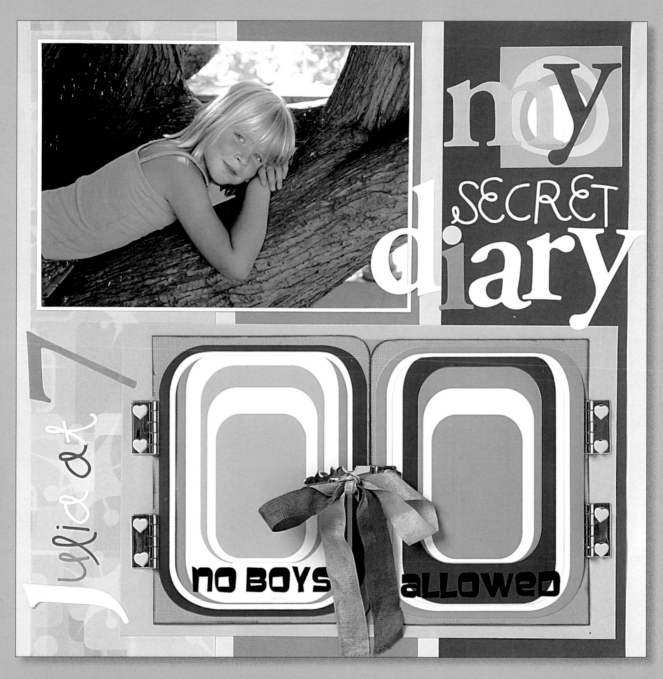

MY SECRET DIARY: by Ann-Marie Weis
Supplies *Patterned paper and cardstock stickers:* Sassafras Lass; *Ribbon:* 7gypsies; *Letter stickers:* American Crafts; *Brads:* Bazzill Basics Paper; *Hinges and clasp:* Ives Schlage.

IDEA TO NOTE: Ann-Marie made a little diary with hinged doors and asked her daughter to write several of her secrets inside of the diary.

LAZY 5 RANCH: by Candace Leonard
Supplies *Cardstock and patterned paper:* KI Memories; *Hinges, brads and paint:* Making Memories; *Tile:* Junkitz; *Rub-ons:* Craf-T Products; *Stamps:* Postmodern Design and Li'l Davis Designs, *Stamping ink:* Memories, Stewart Superior Corporation; *Font:* 2Peas Renaissance, downloaded from *www.twopeasinabucket.com*.

IDEA TO NOTE: Candace added mini-books for extra photographs and journaling to her page by attaching pieces of cardstock to her layout with hinges.

DRIVERS IN TRAINING: by Jenn Brookover
Supplies *Textured cardstock and brads:* Bazzill Basics Paper; *Patterned paper:* Chatterbox; *Transparency:* Art Warehouse, Creative Imaginations; *Fabric paper:* Michael Miller; *Title letters:* Making Memories (mailbox letter) and Li'l Davis Designs (chipboard); *Hinges and date stamp:* Making Memories; *Ribbon:* May Arts (red), C.M. Offray & Son (black and white checked), Memories (white with black); *Corner rounder:* Creative Memories; *Tag die cut:* Sizzix; *Letter stamps:* PSX Design; *Stamping ink:* VersaColor, Tsukineko; *Computer font:* Century Gothic, Microsoft Word; *Other:* Key.

Attaching metal accents

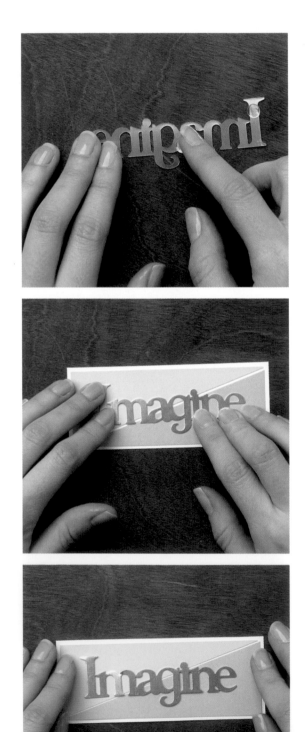

Metal embellishments are eye-catching for their dimension, weight and slick surfaces. But, they can be troublesome to adhere because of those same features. Never fear! With this technique, you'll soon be affixing plaques, tiles, dog tags and more onto your layouts with security and ease.

Step 1:
■ Place the accent face down on a flat surface.

Step 2:
■ Dab the back with metal glue or apply several adhesive dots. For larger items, use metal glue or double-stick tape. Use dimensional foam tape for added height.

Step 3:
■ Flip over and press gently onto background. If using metal glue, hold firmly for a few seconds to set.

Supplies *Metal word:* Making Memories.

KK GIRL: by Angelia Wigginton
Supplies *Patterned paper:* KI Memories; *Vellum:* The Paper Company; *Ribbon:* 7gypsies and me & my BIG ideas; *Eyelets, bookplates, small tag, metal word, metal letter, metal tag, acrylic paint, foam stamps and photo corners:* Making Memories; *Epoxy word:* Creative Imaginations; *Jump rings and button:* Junkitz; *Stamping ink:* Hero Arts.

Jordan, you are one

Cool Dude

You are such a fun little boy. You constantly make me laugh. And I love to laugh! Like today when you casually walked up to me and started talking about something very ordinary, with a pair of sunglasses on and a hat turned cock-eyed. Or what about the time you were dressed in a parka, 2 hats, missing shoe and an orange cone on your hand...in the dead of summer? Yep.

You are a silly little boy. You pull off dorkiness so well. You are probably the only kid I know that could walk into a room wearing sunglasses with gold lenses and a cock-eyed hat, and still look cool...but that's just you. That's just my Jordan... you are one cool dude!

SEP 0 4 2004

ONE COOL DUDE: by Teri Fode
Supplies *Patterned papers:* Karen Foster Design and Sandylion; *Metal letters:* Provo Craft; *Metal tag, staples, molding strips and ribbon:* Making Memories; *Transparency:* OfficeMax; *Acrylic paint:* Delta Technical Coatings and Making Memories; *Label maker:* Dymo; *Brads:* Doodlebug Design; *Computer font:* Papyrus, Microsoft Word.

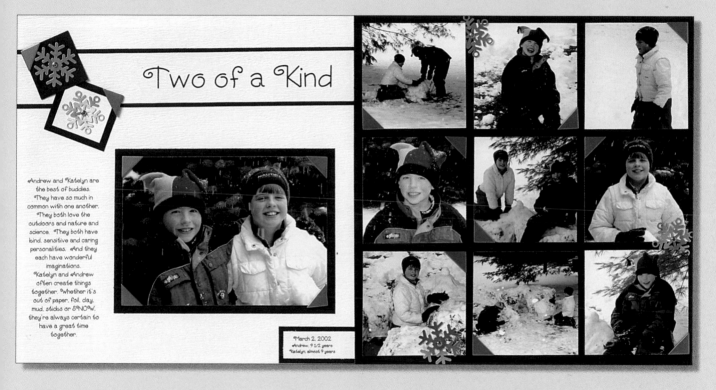

Two of a Kind

Andrew and Katelyn are the best of buddies. They have so much in common with one another. They both love the outdoors and nature and science. They both have kind, sensitive and caring personalities. And they each have wonderful imaginations. Katelyn and Andrew often create things together. Whether it's out of paper, foil, clay, mud, sticks or SNOW, they're always certain to have a great time together.

March 2, 2002
Andrew, 9 1/2 years
Katelyn, almost 9 years

TWO OF A KIND: by Sally Garrod
Supplies *Metal snowflakes, brads and photo corners:* Making Memories; *Computer font:* CK Curly, "The Best of Creative Lettering" CD Combo, *Creating Keepsakes.*

Attaching pressed flowers and leaves

Beautiful. Natural. Delicate. Real pressed flowers and leaves provide layouts with a fresh burst of color and add the perfect textural touch for wedding, outdoor and seasonal pages. Adhering them, however, can be tricky since they easily flake, crack and tear. Try the following tricks to keep them looking as good as the day they were picked:

Step 1:
■ Flip the flower (or leaf) over so its veins are facing up.

Step 2:
■ Dot liquid adhesive sparingly to the veins and heavier portions of the flower. (Hint: Avoid bending the flower.)

Step 3:
■ Press gently onto the background, using a scrap of paper to blot any excess adhesive.

VARIATION • • • *You can also apply a light coat of spray adhesive or a few adhesive dots. Remove the dots from the roll before applying them to the flower. Applying the dots directly from the roll to the flower may tear the petals or crack the leaves.*

Supplies *Pressed flowers and leaf:* Colorbök.

living in a fairy tale

the first time Jeremy saw these pictures he said, "You look like you're in a fairy tale." I replied, "I feel like I'm in one!" I'm just so happy with the life God has blessed me with. He sent me the man of my dreams followed by my little angel. I love getting to spend all day with Mal at home, then wait for Jeremy by the window. It's everything I always wanted... my little *fairy tale*

LIVING IN A FAIRY TALE: by Megan Jones
Supplies *Textured cardstock:* Bazzill Basics Paper; *Dried flowers:* Oh Naturale; *Pens:* Gelly Roll, Sakura; *Photo corners:* Making Memories; *Other:* Fibers.

IDEA TO NOTE: Megan adhered the dried flowers to her layout with a small amount of liquid adhesive.

Attaching a watch crystal

Watch crystals are an ideal way to create instant shakers or to showcase tiny photos, pre-made accents or other embellishments. Trapping accents beneath the glass—or plastic, if you're cautious about using the real thing on your page—is a sure-fire way to get them noticed, as long as sloppy gobs of adhesive don't get in the way. Here's how to keep your accent crystal clear.

Step 1:
■ Flip the crystal over with the rim facing up.

Step 2:
■ Using a fine-tipped applicator or toothpick, apply a clear-drying liquid adhesive sparingly around the rim.

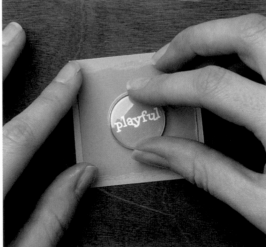

Step 3:
■ Press gently onto the background and hold firmly for a few seconds.

Step 4:
■ Use a toothpick or embossing stylus to remove any excess adhesive that has oozed from the sides.

Supplies *Watch crystal and punch out:* Scrapworks.

Madisann

My beautiful Madisann You are truly a unique individual, and I love you for it. You are spunky, full of life, Energetic, and very loving. You have a one of a kind personality that sets you apart from the rest of the world. I love that you can bring a smile to anyone's face with your silly jokes and facial expressions. Your goal in life is to make sure everyone is happy, which is probably why you want to be a clown when you grow up. While e everyone else dreams of being doctors and firefighters, you have stayed true to your dream of being a clown! Whatever you do you will do it well, especially a clown. The most special thing about you is that you have another wonderful side to your personality, you have the most generous and giving heart. You are always aware of people and their feelings, you are very in tune to the world around us and I think that is a very precious gift that you possess. Madisann, I love you, and cherish who you are. Be true, Be you.

BEST FRIENDS · pLay · LOVE · MY HERO · CAPTURE THE JOY · EXPLORE · reMeMbeR · CELEBRATE LIFE · WITH ALL MY HEART · LIFE · things i love about you

your GROOVE thing

SHAKE YOUR GROOVE THING, YEAH YEAH!

MADISANN: by Jamie Harper
Supplies *Textured cardstock:* Bazzill Basics Paper; *Patterned and embossed papers:* K & Company; *Watch crystals:* Scrapworks; *Adhesive:* Gesso; *Computer fonts:* Scriptina, downloaded from the Internet; Times New Roman, Microsoft Word.

IDEA TO NOTE: To create the custom photo accents on her page, Jamie slipped photographs under watch crystals. Jamie adhered the photographs with gesso, which will dry clear underneath the glass.

SHAKE YOUR GROOVE THING: by Gillian Nelson
Supplies *Textured cardstock:* Bazzill Basics Paper; *Patterned paper:* Paperfever; *Watch crystals and spiral clips:* Scrapworks; *Letter stickers:* Doodlebug Design and Chatterbox; *Labels:* Dymo; *Song lyrics:* "Shake Your Groove Thing" by Peaches & Herb; *Pen:* Slick Writer, American Crafts; *Other:* Letter beads.

IDEA TO NOTE: Gillian's title actually "shakes" to go along with her page theme. To create her title, Gillian glued her spiral clips to her cardstock with the Diamond Glaze adhesive to the cardstock. She then dropped a letter bead in the center area of each clip and glued a watch crystal over the top of each clip.

Attaching micro beads

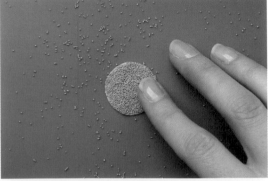

There's nothing like a hint of shimmer to draw your eye to an element. With a dusting of silver, gold or clear micro beads, ordinary accents get an extra helping of glitz and glamour. Discover how a little addition can make a dramatic impact.

Step 1:
■ Completely coat the top of your accent with adhesive. An adhesive sheet, spray or double-stick tape work well. (Hint: To adhere beads to small portions of your accent, coat that area with liquid glue and allow to dry until tacky.)

Step 2:
■ Place the accent into a shallow pan or box frame.

Step 3:
■ Pour micro beads over the accent. To coat completely, turn it face down into the pan (now filled with excess micro beads) and press firmly. Flip it over and press again with your fingertips (or roll over it with a brayer) to further embed the beads. (Hint: To seal the beads, coat the accent with a clear-drying glaze.)

Supplies *Punch outs:* Scrapworks; *Micro beads:* Mark Enterprises.

Skagit Valley Tulip Festival

April 2003

SKAGIT VALLEY TULIP FESTIVAL: by Diane Garding
Supplies *Tulip and daffodil accents:* Diane's own designs; *Beads, tacky tape and glitter:* Provo Craft; *Computer font:* PC Casual, "Never a Dull Moment" CD, Provo Craft.

IDEA TO NOTE: Diane created the tulip accents on her layouts with tacky tape, micro beads and microfine glitter.

AUGUST 2004: by Jennifer Gallacher
Supplies *Patterned paper:* Chatterbox; *Ribbon:* C.M. Offray & Son; *Mini tags:* Avery; *Buckle and rub-on letters:* Li'l Davis Designs; *Safety pin:* Making Memories; *Other:* Beads.

august 2004

Customizing pre-made accents

Unlike stickers, punch outs and other pre-made accents require a little extra effort to adhere; but not much. With a few quick steps, these embellishments can add interest and dimension to any layout.

Step 1:
■ Add any "extras" to customize your accent to match your page theme.

Step 2:
■ Place the accent face down on a flat surface. Place adhesive tabs, dots or double-stick tape on the back. (Hint: If using liquid adhesive, apply sparingly to avoid warping.)

Step 3:
■ Press onto background and smooth with fingertips to flatten.

Supplies *Punch-out:* Sassafrass Lass; *Buttons:* Doodlebug Designs; *Ribbon:* C.M. Offray & Son; *Computer font:* LD Dainty, downloaded from the Internet

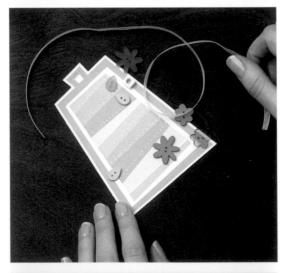

AT THE SEA: by Sally Garrod

Supplies *Stitched paper, border, photo corners and tag:* Paper Bliss, Westrim Crafts; *Vellum:* Provo Craft; *Embroidery floss:* DMC; *Poem:* "At The Sea," by Robert Louis Stevenson; *Computer font:* Papyrus, Microsoft Word.

birthday
W I S H

AGE 5

In Brazil, a child's earlobe is pulled on their birthday for each year she has been alive. The children in Canada have their nose greased, so they will be too slippery for bad luck to catch them. Ireland children are lifted upside down and bumped up and down on the floor. The number of times is determined by the age of the child. Puerto Rican children get taps on the arm, and Scottish children get a soft smack for each year. I like the American tradition the best. Candles are placed on the cake and lit. The child makes a wish and blows out the candles. If they are blown out with one blow, the birthday wish comes true. On your fifth birthday, I'm happy to say. Your wish came true.

ican tradition ● an american tradition ● an american tradition ● an american tradition ● an am

rex

my constant companion

04

loyal smart friend

fun sweet silly brave

friendly kind you

BIRTHDAY WISH: by Lee Anne Russell
Supplies *Textured cardstock:* Bazzill Basics Paper; *Pre-made accents:* KI Memories; *Zipper pulls and letter buttons:* Junkitz; *Rub-ons:* Doodlebug Design; *Chalk:* Deluxe Designs; *Brads:* Making Memories; *Embroidery floss:* DMC; *Other:* Dimensional adhesive.

IDEA TO NOTE: To add color to her zipper pulls, Lee Anne sanded them, chalked them and sealed them with a layer of Crystal Lacquer.

REX: by Candace Leonard
Supplies *Textured cardstock and patterned paper, rub-ons, die cuts and acrylic accents:* KI Memories; *Foam stamps and acrylic paint:* Making Memories; *Computer font:* 2Peas Tigertails, downloaded from *twopeasinabucket.com.*

Attaching ribbon and fiber

Whether you want to tie, hang, weave or attach, there's most likely a length of ribbon, fiber, thread, floss, twill tape, raffia or jute to suit your layout's color and style. Thinner strands can be used in hand stitching, and thicker varieties can be printed on and stamped. And, each can be custom colored with chalk, ink, dye or paint! Following are two basic methods to attach them:

Variation 1:
■ For a flat finish, attach long strands by stringing them across the layout and taping the ends down in back. Ends can also be threaded through slits cut with a craft knife or wound around brads or other fasteners.

Variation 2:
■ For added dimension, wrap ribbon around the back of the project (or bring it up through two holes set with eyelets) and knot in front. (Hint: To keep the ribbon or fiber from shifting, tack it down with adhesive dots or dabs of liquid adhesive.)

Supplies *Ribbon:* May Arts.

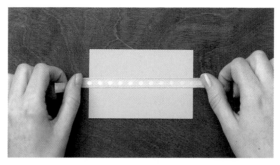

COLORS: by Heather Preckel
Supplies *Textured cardstock:* Bazzill Basics Paper; *Ribbon:* C.M. Offray & Son; *Tag:* Avery; *Rubber stamp:* Postmodern Design; *Brads and rub-ons:* Making Memories; *Photo turns:* 7gypsies; *Label:* Dymo; *Stamping ink:* Ranger Industries; *Computer font:* Stamp Act, downloaded from *www.scrapvillage.com.*

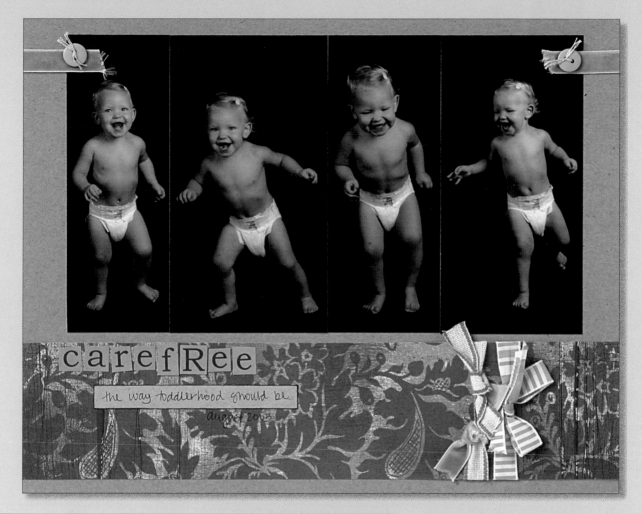

CAREFREE: by Kim Heffington
Supplies *Patterned papers:* BasicGrey (floral) and Mustard Moon (letters); *Ribbon:* Memory Lane; *Button:* Chatterbox; *Stamping ink:* Memories, Stewart Superior Corporation; *Pen:* Slick Writer, American Crafts; *Thread:* Making Memories.

IDEA TO NOTE: Kim tied the strips of ribbon on her border before adhering it to her layout.

ALOHA: by Vanessa Reyes
Supplies *Textured cardstock:* Bazzill Basics Paper; *Patterned paper:* KI Memories; *Title letters:* Li'l Davis Designs (A, L and O) and Mustard Moon (H); *Ribbon:* C.M. Offray & Sons and Wrights; *Stamping ink:* ColorBox, Clearsnap; *Pen:* Zig Writer, EK Success.

IDEA TO NOTE: Vanessa incorporated an actual puzzle piece in her title, painting it white and then stamping the letter "O" onto the piece.

Attaching wire

Flexible, lightweight craft wire is easy to twist, shape, string and attach, once you know the tricks. Because they can snag easily, you'll want to tack wire words and formed shapes securely to your page to prevent them from being, literally, bent out of shape.

Step 1:
■ Attach long strands by using a paper piercer to poke two small holes into the cardstock. Push the ends of the wire through, twisting in back to secure.

Step 2:
■ To keep wire from shifting (or to secure wire shapes), use a paper piercer to poke a tiny hole beneath the wire.

Step 3:
■ Bring a strand of fishing line—knotted in back— through the hole, around the wire, then back down through the same hole. Pull tight, then repeat in several places along the length of wire.

L.I.G.H.T. PARTY: by Kelly Lautenbach
Supplies *Patterned paper:* 7gypsies; *Wire:* Hobby Lobby; *Computer fonts:* AL Surfboard and Sandra, "Handwritten" CD, AL Evening Stroll and AL Updated Classic, "Essential" CD, Autumn Leaves.

IDEA TO NOTE: Notice how Kelly used wire curls to attach the photographs and journaling strips to her layout.

TRUE FRIENDS: by Christy Tomlinson
Supplies *Textured cardstock:* Bazzill Basics Paper; *Patterned papers:* Chatterbox (blue) and KI Memories (pink); *Flower accent:* Prima; *Ribbon:* May Arts, Making Memories and C.M. Offray & Son; *Beads:* Provo Craft; *Rub-ons:* Chatterbox; *Stamping ink:* ColorBox, Clearsnap; *Other:* Staples, charm and craft wire.

IDEA TO NOTE: Create a unique page border by stringing mini-beads and tying coordinating ribbons across thin pieces of fine wire.

Attaching vellum and transparencies

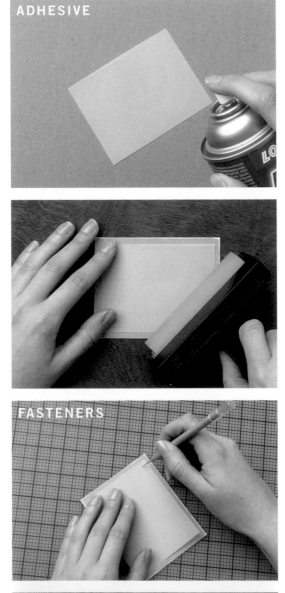

ADHESIVE

FASTENERS

With cool translucent color or crystal clear shine, vellum and transparencies can run the gamut from overlays to delicately layered designs. They're flawless and durable (don't hesitate to use these materials for heat embossing, printing or stamping), but nothing can mar their finish more quickly that telltale adhesive streaks. Try one of the following options for mess-free results:

WITH ADHESIVE

Step 1:
■ Completely cover the back with a light coat of spray adhesive, face up. (Hint: Adhesive may cause slight cloudiness.)

Step 2:
■ Position carefully before pressing (pressing and lifting may cause the material to wrinkle or the adhesive to streak). Press piece down, smoothing with fingers or a burnisher.

WITH FASTENERS

Step 1:
■ Position the material. Holding the vellum/transparency and background together, punch a small hole at the corner using a ⅛" punch.

Step 2:
■ Insert an eyelet or brad through both pieces and flatten. (Hint: See the eyelet and brad setting techniques on pages 104 and 107 for further hints on using the fasteners.)

Supplies *Brad and snap:* Making Memories; *Concho:* Colorbök.

BY OVERLAPPING

Step 1:

■ Arrange elements on your accent or page, positioning them so at least one item covers a portion of the vellum/transparency.

Step 2:

■ Use double-stick tape (or other adhesive) to adhere the portion of the vellum/transparency that will be covered. Secure from the top, as well, by placing additional adhesive on the element overlapping it. (Hint: Even if the transparent piece isn't adhered completely, it will most likely lie flat when inside a page protector.)

Supplies *Patterned paper:* KI Memories.

OVERLAPPING

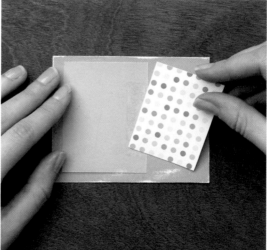

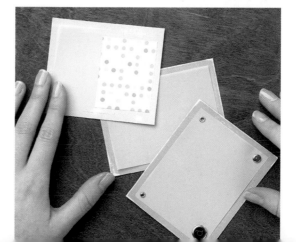

The Red Trike

um·mer'

I was so excited to buy Cole his very own trike this summer! I have fond memories of my own trike, and I wanted Cole to be able to have those happy memories, too. So one weekend in May we dropped by Toys R' Us and picked out the very last retro red Radio Flyer that they had in stock. Since its purchase Cole has taken many rides on his trike, and the shininess has worn off and given way to a few dents and scratches. Though he has yet to use the pedals consistently, I know he'll soon be pedaling with ease, with his feet whirling as quickly as life seems to speed on by. As I stand and watch him play, I am so thankful that we are able to provide for Cole those kinds of memories and milestones that I treasure from my own childhood. 10.04

THE RED TRIKE: by Joanna Bolick
Supplies *Textured cardstock:* Bazzill Basics Paper; *Patterned paper:* Li'l Davis Designs; *Transparency:* Narratives, Creative Imaginations; Daisy D's Paper Paper Co.; *Computer font:* American Typewriter, downloaded from the Internet.

THEN AND NOW: by Heather Preckel
Supplies *Textured cardstock:* Bazzill Basics Paper; *Patterned papers:* 7gypsies (pink) and Rusty Pickle (brown); *Transparency:* K & Company; *Clock hands:* Anima Designs; *Clock faces:* 7gypsies; *Ribbon:* Michaels (brown) and C.M. Offray & Son (gingham); *Brads and twill letters:* Carolee's Creations; *Letter stickers:* FoofaLa; *Computer font:* Old Typewriter, downloaded from the Internet.

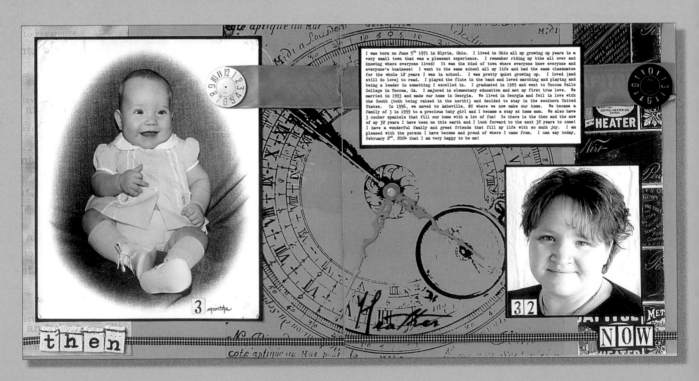

I was born on June 5th 1971 in Elyria, Ohio. I lived in Ohio all my growing up years in a very small town that was a pleasant experience. I remember riding my bike all over and knowing where everyone lived! It was the kind of town where everyone knew everyone and everyone's business! I went to the same school all my life and had the same classmates for the whole 12 years I was in school. I was pretty quiet growing up. I loved (and still do love) to read. I played the flute in the band and loved marching and playing and being a leader in something I excelled in. I graduated in 1989 and went to Toccoa Falls College in Toccoa, GA. I majored in elementary education and met my first true love. We married in 1993 and made our home in Georgia. We lived in Georgia and fell in love with the South (both being raised in the north!) and decided to stay in the southern United States. In 1996, we moved to Asheville, NC where we now make our home. We became a family of 3 in 1999 to a precious baby girl and I became a stay at home mom. We also have 3 cocker spaniels that fill our home with a lot of fun! So there is the then and the now of my 32 years I have been on this earth and I look forward to the next 32 years to come! I have a wonderful family and great friends that fill my life with so much joy. I am pleased with the person I have become and proud of where I came from. I can say today, February 2nd, 2004 that I am very happy to be me!

then

NOW

SENTIMENTAL TREASURE: by Elizabeth Ruuska

Supplies *Patterned paper:* 7gypsies; *Vellum:* Autumn Leaves and Cloud 9 Design; *Beads:* Blue Moon Beads, Creativity Inc.; *Pins:* Making Memories; *Computer font:* Carpenter, downloaded from the Internet.

IDEA TO NOTE: To create the focal point of her layout (the ballerina), Elizabeth first printed the photograph of the ballerina on cardstock. She layered colored printed vellum over the top of the ballerina picture. Finally, she printed the ballerina picture again, tearing portions of it so that the face and torso are prominent.

Using a paper punch

Like die cuts on a miniature scale, paper punches can instantly produce precision shapes out of cardstock, patterned paper, specialty paper and thin metal sheets. Available in an array of detailed shapes and sizes, punches can be used to adorn mats, journaling and title blocks, while their negative spaces can serve as quick, custom stencils or shaker frames. Coat them with leafing pens as faux metallic charms, recolor them with paint or ink, string them together or use them in shaker boxes—above all, give them a try.

Step 1:
■ Insert cardstock (or other flat material) into the underside of the punch, in the opening just above the bottom metal plate.

Step 2:
■ Using your palm or thumb (depending on the size of the punch), firmly press down on the lever until the punch cuts through the cardstock. (Hint: A device like the Power Punch can make intricate punches easier to use. Occasionally punching through wax paper and aluminum foil will keep your punches lubricated and sharpened.)

Supplies *Punch:* EK Success.

Using a die cut machine

As one of scrapbooking's original embellishment options, die cuts can support any layout theme with shapes that celebrate most holidays, seasons and occasions. With a little creativity and some basic supplies, they evolve from simple shapes to embellished masterpieces. Whether you're creating die cuts from cardstock, patterned or specialty paper, it's as easy as 1-2-3.

PERSONAL

Step 1:

■ Place cardstock (or other material) onto the white cutting pad.

Step 2:

■ Place a die, face down, over the cardstock.

Step 3:

■ Slide the pad under the press and push the lever down firmly two or three times to ensure a crisp cut.

VARIATION • • • *Hand-held die cut tools operate much like hole punches. Position the metal die and cardstock on the plate and press the handles together to cut the shape.*

MY GIRL: by Kristi Baumgarten
Supplies *Textured cardstock:* Bazzill Basics Paper; *Die cuts and letter stickers:* KI Memories; *Ribbon:* Textured Trios, May Arts and Midori; *Flower brad:* Making Memories; *Stamping ink:* ColorBox, Clearsnap; *Pen:* American Crafts; *Other:* Staples.

FOR THE LOVE OF THE GAME: By Vanessa Reyes
Supplies *Textured cardstock:* Bazzill Basics Paper; *Patterned paper, rub-ons, tacks and frame:* Chatterbox; *Die cuts:* Li'l Davis Designs; *Letter stickers:* Wordsworth; *Pen:* Zig Millennium, EK Success.

Using tags

It's no wonder that tags have become such popular page accents...whether pre-printed or plain, they can serve as mini canvases for unlimited looks or as decorative mats for titles, photos, journaling and more. Available in an array of sizes and materials, you'll learn to rely on tags for instant dimension, texture or eye-catching interest.

Step 1:

■ Select a pre-cut tag or use a template, die cut machine or punch to generate one. (Hint: Think beyond cardstock – try cork, metal, fabric, specialty paper and other surfaces to create tags.) If desired, enhance the tag with decoupage, mesh or by coloring with paint, ink, rub-ons or chalks.

Step 2:

■ Adorn with photos, text, or embellishments such as stickers, pre-made accents, charms and more.

Step 3:

■ Top and attach the tag to your page with ribbon, fibers, bead chain or fasteners such as brads, staples or conchos.

Supplies *Textured paper:* Provo Craft; *Tag:* Avery; *Acrylic paint:* Making Memories (orange and green), Delta Technical Coatings (black); *Fiber:* EK Success; *Acrylic letters:* KI Memories; *Brad and embroidery floss:* Making Memories; *Transparency:* Hammermill; *Other:* Clip.

JUST YOUR GARDEN VARIETY BOY: by Patricia Anderson
Supplies *Textured cardstock:* Bazzill Basics Paper; *Patterned paper and tags:* Rusty Pickle; *Word tags and mini brads:* Making Memories; *Acrylic paint:* DecoArt; *Computer fonts:* Antique Type and Hootie, downloaded from the Internet; CBX-Heber, Journaling Font CD, Chatterbox.

IDEA TO NOTE: Patricia created her title by typing it in Word Art. She reversed the text, printed it on cardstock and handcut it with scissors.

Using stickers

This scrapbooking staple has evolved right along with the craft of scrapbooking. Now available in updated styles and cardstock, dimensional, photo, paper-pieced, epoxy, metal, cork and leather varieties, stickers are still a fast and fashionable way to embellish layouts.

Step 1:

■ Peel backing from sticker and press onto layout. (Hint: To add dimension to "flat" stickers, powder the self-adhesive with corn starch to remove stickiness, then adhere to the background with foam tape instead.)

VARIATIONS • • • *Create sticker scenes by mixing and matching designs; use pieces in decoupage and collage; utilize alphabet stickers for title lettering and journaling; distress shiny stickers by sanding, crumpling or with a bit of ink, paint or color washing; or add highlights with glitter, heat embossing, leafing pens and more.*

Supplies *Sticker:* me & my BIG ideas; *Ribbon:* C.M. Offray & Son

MUD BATH: by Cindy Knowles

Supplies *Vellum:* WorldWin Extraordinary Papers; *Foam stamps and definition stickers:* Making Memories; *Acrylic paint:* Plaid Enterprises; *Letter stamps:* Rubber Stampede; *Stamping ink:* StazOn, Tsukineko; *Library pocket and printed ribbon:* Boxer Scrapbook Productions; *Ribbon:* May Arts; *Paper clips:* EK Success; *Computer font:* Goudy Sans, downloaded from the Internet; *Other:* Film strips.

IDEA TO NOTE: To create the background texture on the cardstock, Cindy dabbed paint through tulle, carpet backing and mesh. Her layout colors match the dried mud on her daughter's face.

intermediate embellishing

4

A sweep of chalk for a subtle tint. Some crumpled cardstock for a hint of texture. A torn edge for a bit of dimension. It's amazing what a few simple touches can do for the artistry, richness and character of a layout. Take a few minutes to learn each of these straightforward techniques—you'll soon discover that a little effort can give your pages a whole new look.

Applying chalk

With a bit of chalk, you can shade, age and tint. With a little effort, you can generate textures, highlights and soft, faux finishes. And with a variety of applicators including cotton balls, swabs, sponges, brushes or your fingertips you can create unlimited looks that range from innocent to industrial.

Step 1:

■ Swipe an applicator across the chalk square, then tap off excess.

Step 2:

■ Rubbing in a circular motion, apply chalk to the desired area. Highlight edges, shade or give the entire piece a subtle tint. (Hint: Build up color by using several light layers rather than trying to add too much color at once.) If you make a mistake, a chalk eraser can remove some of the color.

Step 3:

■ When finished, flip the piece face down onto scrap paper and burnish by rubbing firmly with your fingertips or a brayer or burnisher. This will help "set" the chalk. You can also spray with an acid-free fixative, if desired.

VARIATIONS • • • *Apply chalk with a blender pen for a watercolored look or brush over an image stamped in pigment ink for a velvety effect.*

Supplies *Template:* Pebbles In My Pocket.

CAT ART: by Kelly Lautenbach
Supplies *Patterned paper:* SEI; *Stamping ink:* VersaMark, Tsukineko; *Letter stamps:* FontWerks; *Definition stamp:* Cat's Life Press; *Chalk:* Close To My Heart.

CRIME & PUNISHMENT

ALLIE, I ABOUT DIED ONE DAY WHEN I CAME INTO MY BATHROOM AND SAW A PILE OF HAIR LYING ON THE FLOOR! YOU HAD SUCH LONG BEAUTIFUL HAIR AND YOU HAD JUST GIVEN YOURSELF A MULLET. I WAS SO UPSET WITH YOU! I TOOK YOU TO THE HAIR SALON TO SEE IF THEY COULD "FIX" IT SOMEHOW, AND THE WOMAN TOLD US THE ONLY THING SHE COULD DO WAS CUT IT ALL OFF. YOU WERE CRYING, I WAS CRYING. NOW MY ONLY DAUGHTER, LOOKED JUST LIKE THE REST OF MY FOUR BOYS! I KNEW IT WOULD GROW BACK BUT THAT DIDN'T SEEM TO MAKE ME FEEL ANY BETTER. THE HAIRDRESSER SUGGESTED PIERCING YOUR EARS TO HELP YOU LOOK MORE LIKE A GIRL. YOUR EYES GOT REALLY WIDE AND A BIG GRIN APPEARED ON YOUR FACE! YOU HAD BEEN ASKING ME FOR MONTHS TO GET YOUR EARS PIERCED. BUT I THOUGHT YOU WERE TOO YOUNG AND NEEDED TO WAIT A FEW MORE YEARS. I DIDN'T KNOW WHAT TO DO, BUT WE ENDED UP PIERCING YOUR EARS ANYWAY. WHEN WE GOT HOME, YOU RAN INTO THE HOUSE TO SHOW DAD YOUR NEW EARRINGS! YOU TOLD HIM, I GOT INTO TROUBLE BECAUSE I CUT MY HAIR AND SO MOM LET ME GET MY EARS PIERCED! YOUR DAD JUST LOOKED AT ME AND SMILED. "WELL SWEETS", HE SAID... "IT LOOKS LIKE YOU GOT A REALLY BAD PUNISHMENT." YEAH RIGHT!

yeah right!

Caleb is so full of life and energy and loves to be on the go. His energy level is overwhelming at times. Despite this, there are some activities and adventures that cause him a little trepidation. Although sometimes it is puzzling that he doesn't just jump in and try everything because of his natural exuberance, I am very grateful for his reservations at times... otherwise we might spend a lot of time in the emergency room!

Spirit of Adventure
caleb style

CRIME AND PUNISHMENT: by Christy Tomlinson
Supplies *Textured cardstock:* Bazzill Basics Paper; *Patterned papers:* KI Memories and Chatterbox; *Handmade paper:* Artistic Scrapper, Creative Imaginations; *Rubber stamps:* Kai Mae and Making Memories; *Rub-ons:* Chatterbox; *Flower accent:* Prima; *Ribbon:* May Arts and Making Memories; *Safety pins:* Making Memories; *Chalk:* Craf-T Products; *Stamping ink:* VersaMark, Tsukineko; Distressed Ink, Ranger Industries; *Computer font:* 2Peas Tasklist, downloaded from www.twopeasinabucket.com.

SPIRIT OF ADVENTURE: by Darcee Waddoups
Supplies *Stickers:* Chatterbox; *Computer font:* CK Typeset, Becky Higgins' "Creative Clips and Fonts" CD, *Creating Keepsakes; Chalk:* Deluxe Designs; *Pen:* Pigma Micron, Sakura.

Applying metallic rub-ons

Whether it's a simple gilded edge or a solid metal accent, the metallic shine adds an opulent touch that other looks can't. And with metallic rub-ons, these looks are yours whether you're just aiming for a subtle highlight or hoping to give a plain accent a completely metallic transformation.

Step 1:

■ Swipe an applicator or fingertip along the pot of rub-ons. Press lightly on scrap paper to remove excess.

Step 2:

■ Swirl the color on, applying additional coats for a more dramatic finish. (Hint: Smearing rub-ons onto crumpled or textured materials will dramatically emphasize the dimension.)

Step 3:

■ When finished, flip the piece face down onto scrap paper and burnish by rubbing firmly with your fingertips, a brayer or burnisher to help "set" the rub-ons.

VARIATIONS • • • *Apply metallic rub-ons to a variety of surfaces—cardstock, patterned paper, fabric, clay, chipboard tiles, acrylics and more. When applying rub-ons to non-porous surfaces, coat with a clear-drying glaze to set.*

Supplies *Metallic rub-ons:* Craf-T Products.

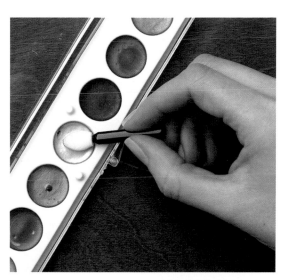

Gracie & Ayden, all dressed up for Ryan and Kristen's wedding reception we couldn't get enough pictures of the cute cousins... they were adorable!
June 24, 2004

COUSINS: by Hilary Shirley
Supplies *Metallic rub-ons:* Craf-T Products; *Staples, jigsaw letter, metal photo corners and ribbon:* Making Memories; *Acrylic paint:* Delta Technical Coatings; *Eyelets:* Doodlebug Design; *Fixative:* Krylon; *Computer font:* Little Days, downloaded from the Internet.

IDEA TO NOTE: Notice how Hilary created her background page by stacking three strips of paper on top of each other. The bottom strip is crumpled, the middle strip is accordion folded and the top strip was left plain. To add shine and texture to her background, Hilary transferred a metallic rub-on to the paper and then sprayed it with a fixative to keep it from smearing.

HARVEST: by Michelle Tardie
Supplies *Textured cardstock:* Bazzill Basics Paper; *Patterned cardstock and die cut:* My Mind's Eye; *Corrugated paper:* Creative Imaginations; *Metallic rub-ons:* Craf-T Products; *Rub-ons:* Making Memories; *Glue dots:* Glue Dots International; *Computer font:* CK Flip Serif, "Clips & Fonts for Special Occasions" CD, *Creating Keepsakes; Other:* Silk flower.

IDEA TO NOTE: To add extra depth to the silk leaf on her page, Michelle transferred a metallic rub-on to the leaf's surface.

FAST: by Kelly Lautenbach
Supplies *Textured cardstock:* Bazzill Basics Paper; *Metallic rub-ons:* Craf-T Products; *Pen:* Zig Writer, EK Success; *Letter stamps:* FontWerks.

Color blocking

Want to create a custom background that suits the color scheme and tone of your layout? Design your own sleek pattern with a paper trimmer and scraps of card-stock. Mix and match colors, crumple a few of the pieces or adhere some with foam tape to turn the simple patterns into even more of a visual treat.

Step 1:
■ Select two or more colors of cardstock.

Step 2:
■ Determine the size of your finished product, then calculate how big each section should be. Trim the cardstock accordingly.

Step 3:
■ Adhere in a uniform fashion to create a straight colorblocked background, either by butting the pieces up next to one another or by leaving space between them.

VARIATIONS • • • *Vary the size of each segment or the materials used to create them. And, though it's not technically "color blocking," use cardstock to design other custom backgrounds. Try stripes, woven strips or patterns with different shapes.*

Work Hard.

much throughout his life; he had to work for it.

Do the Right Thing.

he met had value

Many People have less than we do.

Be Generous

to help at church and school. Be giving of yourself and it will come back to you tenfold

Have Faith.

his Commandments and your life will be full and joyous.

Think Positive.

try
grow
live

FROM PAPA TO GRANT

LIFE Lessons

LIFE LESSONS: by Mary Larson

Supplies *Patterned paper and "life" sticker:* Art Warehouse, Creative Imaginations; *Negative strips:* Narratives, Creative Imaginations; *Ribbon and embroidery floss:* Making Memories; *Mesh:* Magic Mesh; *Word buttons:* K & Company; *Label:* Dymo; *Computer font:* CK Carbon Copy, "Fresh Fonts" CD, *Creating Keepsakes; Other:* Twill tape and beads.

Crumpling cardstock

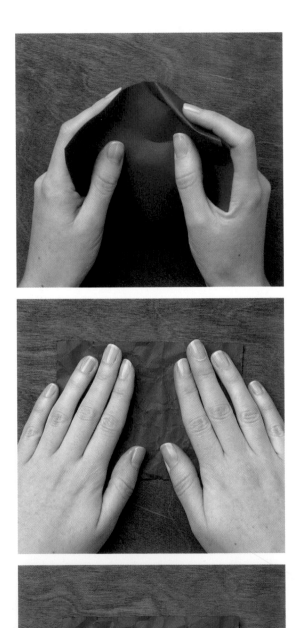

If you thought wadding up paper was a skill that would never come in handy, in the scrapbooking world, you'd be wrong. By crumpling cardstock—carefully, of course—you can add instant interest to backgrounds, photo mats, accents and more.

Step 1:
■ Trim a piece of cardstock slightly larger than the desired size, since it will shrink a bit after crumpling.

Step 2:
■ Work from the outside in, using your fingertips to carefully draw the cardstock in toward your palm. Once it begins to "weaken," you can crumple it more vigorously, even into a ball. (Hint: If the cardstock is tearing significantly, you may want to make some straight folds across the center or mist it with water before crumpling.)

Step 3:
■ Open the paper carefully and smooth flat. For a more even finish, iron the cardstock to flatten.

stories

bedtime

After a crazy, long day of running around, jumping on Opa Rainer's back, finagling Tante Amber into playing card games, feeding pigs and rowing canoes, these two overtired kiddos wanted nothing more than to stay up all night and play with the big-folks. So Mama pulled out a book and gathered them together for one bedtime story using her voice to lull them to complacency and then 'ab die post' and into bed.

April, 2003 -An der Lache

BEDTIME STORIES: by Amber Ries
Supplies *Eyelets:* Making Memories; *Computer fonts:* Antique Type and Franks, downloaded from the Internet.

Decorating a plain slide mount

Slide mounts are perfect for adding a hint of dimension while serving as a mini frame to showcase small photos, text and tiny accents. Customize them to suit your layout's colors and theme by brushing with paint or decorating with stickers or rub-ons. Or resurface them completely with matching patterned paper. Here's how:

Step 1:
■ Trim a piece of patterned paper so it's slightly larger than the slide mount. Use adhesive (such as double-stick tape) to affix the slide mount to the back of the paper.

Step 2:
■ Use a craft knife to cut an "X" into the paper in the center portion of the slide mount. Cut the paper diagonally along the outside corners of the slide mount as well.

Step 3:
■ Apply adhesive to all four sides of the slide mount.

Step 4:
■ Fold the eight flaps (four outer edges, four inner pieces) over the adhesive.

Step 5:
■ Flip the slide mount over and press it with your fingertips to ensure all the edges are adhered.

Supplies *Patterned paper:* Deluxe Designs.

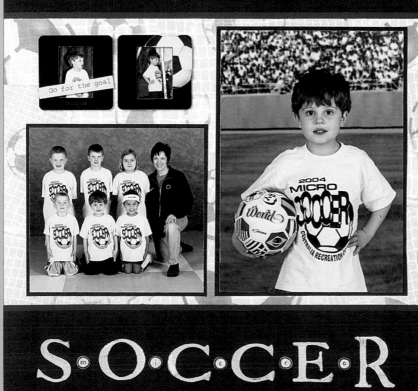

SUPERSTAR: by Marilyn Healey
Supplies *Patterned paper and letter stickers:* Doodlebug Design; *Vellum:* Paper Adventures; *Stamping ink:* ColorBox, Clearsnap; *Star punch:* EK Success; *Computer font:* Doodle Cursive, "Page Printables" CD Vol. 1, Cock-A-Doodle Design; *Other:* Slide frames.

SOCCER: by Heidi Stepanova
Supplies *Patterned paper and stickers:* Karen Foster Design; *Foam stamps and acrylic paint:* Making Memories; *Letter stamps:* PSX Design; *Stamping ink:* ColorBox, Clearsnap; *Slide holders:* Jest Charming; *Clay:* Makins.

Making a photo mosaic

As an artistic treatment for your focal point picture, create a picturesque photo mosaic. With a paper trimmer and some adhesive, you can also turn scrap photos into funky borders, mats or backgrounds for titles, journaling or other snapshots.

Step 1:
■ Select a scenic photo or one with a lot of background surrounding the subject. (Hint: Be sure to have a duplicate photo on hand in case you're unhappy with the results.)

Step 2:
■ Using a paper trimmer or a craft knife and ruler, cut the photo into uniform squares.

Step 3:
■ Reassemble the photo on cardstock, adhering with tabs or dots, leaving space around each piece.

VARIATION • • • *Leave the main subject of the photo intact and trim the background into squares for a mosaic border. Change it up by tilting or using foam tape to elevate some of the pieces.*

DAY TRIPPIN': by Allison Landy
Supplies *Patterned paper:* Daisy D's Paper Paper Co.; *Letter rub-ons:* Making Memories; *Tacks:* Chatterbox; *Pen:* Zig Scroll & Brush, EK Success.

AUSTIN THE GHOST: by Marilyn Healey
Supplies *Patterned paper and shape template:* Provo Craft; *Letter stickers:* me & my BIG ideas; Creative Imaginations; *Label:* Chatterbox; *Brads:* Lost Art Treasures.

Making a shaker box

Give layouts a sense of motion and whimsy by creating shakers out of shaped accents and title lettering or by placing them over photos, journaling and more. Fill with themed accents such as tiny shells, punch pieces and mini buttons, or decorate the transparent "window" with stamps or rub-ons to add even more interest.

Step 1:

■ Choose a "frame" for the shaker—either a die cut, punch out, letter or cardstock shape. Use a craft knife to cut the center away, leaving a narrow outline.

Step 2:

■ Create a "window" by flipping the object over and adhering a piece of transparency over the opening, using tape or liquid adhesive to seal completely.

Step 3:

■ Apply dimensional foam tape to the back of the frame.

Step 4:

■ "Fill" the frame with beads, glitter or other accents. (Hint: If the filling is "sticking" to the window, rub the transparency with an anti-static sheet before adhering.)

Step 5:

■ Invert the background and press it onto the shaker to adhere. (Hint: You can also apply the dimensional tape to your background, place the filling within the taped lines, then press the "window and frame" on top. If you do this, be sure to measure carefully to ensure the adhesive will be beneath the shaker frame.)

VARIATIONS • • • *Try this technique using slide mounts or pre-made frames rather than hand cutting shaker frames.*

Supplies *Template:* Pebbles In My Pocket.

The Cat's Out
of the ~~Bag~~ Box

July 13 2001

Meow

When we adopted Andrei we already had 2 dogs, 2 cats, guinea pigs and a fish tank. He especially loved the cats. We thought it would be a good experience for him to have a kitten so we bought him one for his first birthday here. He named the kitten "Kola", after a friend from the orphanage.

WEYERHAEUSER

Meow   PAW PRINTS   Nine Lives

THE CAT'S MEOW

THE CAT'S OUT OF THE BAG: by Diane Garding
Supplies *Patterned paper:* Eco-African, Provo Craft; *Rub-ons, tag, letter stickers and beads:* Provo Craft; *Cat buttons:* Dress It Up, Jesse James & Co.; *Fiber:* Fibers By The Yard; *Paper clip:* Target; *Computer font:* CK Toggle, "The Best of Creative Lettering" CD Combo, *Creating Keepsakes; Other:* Eyelets, foam strips and button.

Let it snow...let it snow...let it

SNOW!

It had been a wonderful snow season, but little Cooper still hadn't been properly introduced. This Sunday morning a fresh snowfall was so beautiful Mommy dressed baby in a warm snowsuit and took him outside. He loved it!   February 2004

LET IT SNOW: by Jennifer Blackham
Supplies *Patterned paper:* Provo Craft; *Snowflake die cut and beads:* Provo Craft; *Square punch:* EK Success; *Shaved ice:* Magic Scraps; *Foam tape:* 3M; *Computer font:* PC Rat-a-Tat, "A Gathering of Friends" CD, Provo Craft; *Other:* Button.

Paper piecing

For the ultimate in handmade page accents, create a paper-pieced design. If you can trace, cut and glue (and like to assemble puzzles), this may be the technique for you. Recreate patterned paper motifs and elements in your photos or use tole painting patterns, rubber stamps, clip art or coloring books as base designs.

Step 1:
■ Print or copy a pattern and reduce or enlarge to size.

Step 2:
■ Trace each piece onto the desired shade of cardstock or patterned paper and trim. (Hint: If you want to keep your original intact, use vellum or tissue paper to trace each piece. Eliminate a second tracing by placing the tissue over your cardstock and cutting both at the same time.)

Step 3:
■ Assemble the design, adhering the pieces either to the background or to other pieces.

VARIATIONS • • • *Add further definition by chalking, tracing edges with a pen, using textured paper or adhering some pieces with dimensional tape.*

Supplies *Template:* ScrapPagerz.

5 DOLLAR PONY RIDE: by Vanessa Reyes
Supplies *Textured cardstock:* Bazzill Basics Paper; *Patterned paper:* Chatterbox; *Letter stickers:* American Crafts ("pony"), The Paper Loft ("ride"); *Square metal tag:* Making Memories; *Tacks:* Chatterbox; *Letter stamps:* Hero Arts; *Stamping ink:* Stampin' Up!; *Horse and flower paper-piecings:* Vanessa's own designs; *Number sticker:* Creative Imaginations; *Pen:* Zig Writer, EK Success; *Other:* Ribbon and fabric.

ON THE GO: by Jennifer Gallacher
Supplies *Patterned paper:* Cross My Heart; *Letter stamps:* PSX Design; *Stamping ink:* Memories, Stewart Superior Corporation; *Buttons:* Making Memories.

Sanding

Change the face of patterned paper, cardstock and pre-made accents with easy sanding techniques. Using sandpaper, a wire brush or steel wool, just rub, buff or scratch a material's surface to wear it away. In addition to adding a bit of texture, sanding can also age, dull, or soften an element's color.

Step 1:
■ Place the item to be sanded on a piece of white scrap paper. (If you use a piece that's colored, its tint may transfer onto the item you're sanding.)

Step 2:
■ Hold the sandpaper in your dominant hand while holding the item down with the other. Rub the sandpaper against the item with short strokes. The grain of the sandpaper and direction of your sanding can affect the result. While a fine grain will gently distress the surface, a coarse grain can be used in long strokes for a "scratched" look or in two different directions for a "cross-hatch" finish.

Step 3:
■ Use a tissue to wipe away any gritty residue.

Supplies *Patterned paper and punch out:* KI Memories.

FOURTH OF JULY: by Dece Gherardini
Supplies *Patterned papers:* Creative Papers and BasicGrey; *Textured paper:* BazzillBasics Paper; *Ribbon:* Autumn Leaves and C.M. Offray & Son; *Letter stamps:* PSX Design; *Stamping ink:* Rubber Stampede; *Pen:* Permapaque, Sakura; *Brads:* Making Memories.

Tearing paper

Here's a secret. The quickest way to trim cardstock, design a background or size an accent is simply tear it! Create decorative edges in seconds with just your fingertips or the aid of a specially-designed ruler. Achieve diverse looks merely by varying your tearing style.

Variation 1:

■ For a long tear with a wide torn edge, simply grasp the cardstock in the fingertips of both hands and pull them in opposite directions.

Variation 2:

■ For a jagged, but controlled tear, place the cardstock on a flat surface and hold it with one hand while using the thumb and index finger of your other hand to make smaller, slower tears.

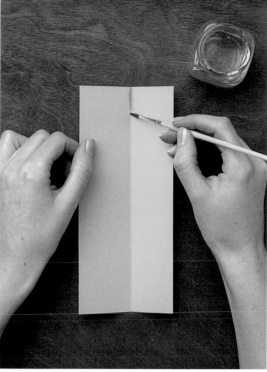

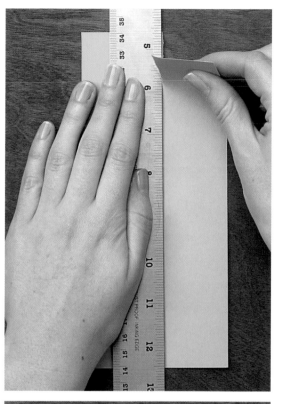

Variation 3:

■ For a straight, slightly fuzzy tear, fold the cardstock, use a Q-tip or paintbrush to apply a line of water to the fold, then pull the two sides apart.

Variation 4:

■ For a quick, straight tear, score the cardstock and hold a ruler securely over the crease. Pull the other side toward you, against the ruler. (Rulers are available with special edges, such as deckle, that will allow you to produce decorative tears with this technique.)

MY STYLE: by Kim Kesti
Supplies *Textured cardstock:* Bazzill Basics Paper; *Patterned paper:* Paperfever; *Letter stickers:* Shotz, Creative Imaginations ("my"); American Crafts ("Style"); *Acrylic paint:* Delta Technical Coatings; *Paper clips:* Target; *Stamping ink:* Ranger Industries.

READ: by Patricia Anderson
Supplies *Textured cardstock:* Prism Papers; *Patterned paper:* KI Memories; *Letter stickers:* American Crafts; *Computer font:* Times New Roman, Microsoft Word; *Tag:* Rusty Pickle.

IDEA TO NOTE: To recreate the book cover on her page, Patricia took a digital photograph of the book, printed it on photo paper and trimmed it to size.

advanced embellishing

5

Do you remember that childhood urge to make a mud pie? That feeling of accomplishment and glee as you fashioned something out of nothing, mud squishing messily through your fingers? Well, it's time to play. Recapture that sensation and unleash your creativity with some advanced, artistic — and occasionally messy — techniques. With the following instructions and a bit of experimentation, you can design your most inventive and inspired pages yet.

Color washing

FABRIC DYE

Add an antique finish, a subtle tint or a completely different hue to cardstock, patterned paper, fabrics, twill tape and more with a simple color wash. Brushing, dipping, spritzing and sponging are all easy ways to apply walnut ink, fabric dyes, paints, coffee, tea and other mediums. Cover your workspace to protect it from drips and try one of these popular methods:

FABRIC DYE

Step 1:

■ Dissolve the powder in tepid water in a shallow pan until the desired color is achieved. (Hint: You can also blend colors to create new shades.)

Step 2:

■ To give the entire piece a subtle tint, submerge it in the liquid, remove immediately and dry on paper towels. (Hint: If the paper is warped, flatten under a heavy book or iron—between two pieces of waxed paper—while still moist. Set your iron on the "acetate" setting.)

VARIATIONS • • • *To create different finishes, drag or press items into the wet paper to texturize—dip just the paper's edges into bowls of dye or apply with a paint brush or a spray bottle. For gradated tints, hold paper by one edge after removing from the dye, allowing it to drip to the bottom.*

Supplies *Patterned paper:* Deluxe Designs; *Dye:* Rit.

WALNUT INK

Step 1:

■ If you have walnut ink crystals, dissolve them according to package instructions or in enough water to achieve the desired shade (more water for lighter color).

Step 2:

■ For a subtle "aged" quality, brush it on in long, even strokes. (Hint: If the paper begins to buckle, flatten under a heavy book or iron lightly.)

VARIATIONS • • • *To completely coat an object, such as a tag, dissolve the crystals in a plastic sandwich bag and submerge the tag in the liquid. For a mottled texture, put dye into a spray bottle and spritz, or dab it on with a sponge or stippling brush.*

Supplies *Patterned paper:* Deluxe Designs.

WATERCOLORS

Step 1:

■ Dip a paint brush in water and swipe along the pot of paint to pick up color. (Hint: Use a drier brush for richer color, more water for a diluted wash. Brush a bit more water on the painted surface to lighten the color even more.)

Step 2:

■ Apply color to paper in swirls, long or short strokes, depending on the finish you'd like to achieve. Allow to dry completely.

VARIATIONS • • • *Color the paper lightly with watercolor pencils and blend the color by washing over it with a wet brush or create a mottled finish by spritzing the paper with water.*

Supplies *Patterned paper:* Deluxe Designs.

BLOWING BUBBLES: by Heather Preckel
Supplies *Textured cardstock:* Bazzill Basics Paper; *Ribbon:* C.M. Offray & Son; *Rubber stamps:* Fontwerks; *Color wash:* 7gypsies and Ranger Industries; *Circle template:* Rounderz, Junkitz; *Other:* Ric Rac.

IDEA TO NOTE: Heather cut circle accents from fabric and color-washed them with pink and green paint.

FRIENDS 4EVER: by Allison Landy
Supplies *Mulberry paper:* Bazzill Basics Paper; *Letter stamps:* Limited Edition Rubberstamps; *Color wash dyes:* Adirondack, Ranger Industries; *Stamping ink:* ColorBox, Clearsnap; *Embossing powder:* Creative Beginnings; *Punches:* McGill (small) and All Night Media (medium); *Tags:* Avery; *Page pebbles:* Making Memories; *Brads:* The Happy Hammer; *Other:* Staples and ribbon.

Using dimensional glue and glaze

Give accents instant shine with a quick coat of a glossy adhesive or glaze. But don't stop there. Designed to retain dimension after drying, these products can also be used to create raised tiles, recessed images and more. All you need is something to cover and a little drying time!

Step 1:
■ Begin with a thick pre-made accent, piece of cardstock or chipboard.

Step 2:
■ To give the item a flat, glossy finish, paint a thin layer of glue across the top.

Step 3:
■ To create a shiny "tile," add a single, thick layer of glue directly from the bottle. (Hint: To prevent air bubbles, store the bottle upside down for a few minutes before working and do not shake it before dispensing.)

VARIATIONS • • • *Use glaze or dimensional glue to fill in frame-style conchos to create imitation typewriter keys or use it to cover photos in mini frames for shiny custom charms. Try spreading a thick layer onto cardstock, allowing it to dry until tacky, then pressing an inked stamp onto the surface to leave a cool impression. Or freehand a design, allow it to dry and cover it with paint or rub-ons for a dimensional accent.*

Supplies *Stamping ink:* ColorBox, Clearsnap, Inc.; *Sticker:* Creative Imaginations.

ME AND THE MOMS: by Ann-Marie Weis
Supplies *Patterned paper, stickers, tacks, frame and window:* Chatterbox; *Ribbon:* May Arts; *Beads:* The Bead Shoppe, Creative Beginnings; *Glitter:* Magic Scraps; *Dimensional adhesive:* Aleene's Paper Glaze, Duncan Enterprises.

IDEA TO NOTE: To add extra interest to the tiles on her page, Ann-Marie covered each tile with Paper Glaze and then sprinkled pink beads and glitter around the edges for a 3-D effect.

AUTUMN: by Shannon Taylor
Supplies *Beads:* Blue Moon Beads, Creativity Inc.; *Copper frames:* Nunn Design; *Dimensional adhesive:* Diamond glaze, JudiKins; *Embossing powder:* Stamping Station; *Copper scrap metal:* Once Upon a Scribble; *Poem:* downloaded from *www.twopeasinabucket.com*; *Chalk:* Craf-T Products; *Adhesive:* Super Tape, Therm O Web; *Computer fonts:* Locked Window Font (title) and Jill (journaling), downloaded from the Internet; *Other:* Burlap and corduroy.

decoupaging accents

If you can use scissors and adhesive, you can decoupage. Design a beautiful, collaged surface that only looks difficult and time-consuming. Incorporate scraps, ephemera and memorabilia into custom finishes that can adorn accents, cards and craft projects.

Step 1:
■Assemble various lightweight materials to collage.

Step 2:
■Cut or tear materials into desired sizes.

Step 3:
■Select a piece and coat the back with adhesive or decoupage medium. Adhere it to the background, using a brayer or burnisher to smooth. Repeat until the entire surface is covered.

Step 4:
■Trim edges.

Step 5:
■Burnish to remove any air bubbles. Brush the entire surface with glossy or matte decoupage medium or glaze.

Supplies *Ephemera:* K & Company.

HOPES: by Lisa Damrosch
Supplies *Patterned paper:* Daisy D's Paper Co.; *Flower accent, jigsaw letters, safety pins and ribbon:* Making Memories; *Buttons:* Junkitz; *Stamping ink:* Tsukineko; *Pop dots:* Zots, Therm O Web; *Decoupage medium:* Mod Podge, Plaid Enterprises; *Embroidery floss:* DMC; *Computer font:* Times New Roman, Microsoft Word; *Other:* Photo corners and thread.

marriage

"Remember, for every fault you find in your mate, you have one just as bad or worse. Be quick to forgive."

-Sherry Ward

Don and Teri
est. 12/15/91

MARRIAGE: by Teri Fode
Supplies *Textured cardstock:* Bazzill Basics Paper; *Letter stickers:* Doodlebug Design; *Ribbon:* C.M. Offray & Son and Li'l Davis Designs; *Stamping ink:* Ranger Industries; *Decoupage medium:* Mod Podge; *Paper clip:* Target; *Computer font:* Times New Roman, Microsoft Word; *Other:* Chipboard.

IDEA TO NOTE: To add interest to her focal photograph, Teri printed it on cardstock and then decoupaged it with three thin layers of Mod Podge.

Dry Embossing

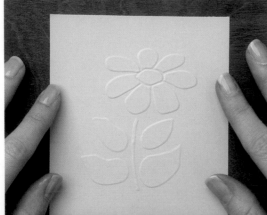

Whether you choose a decorative motif or a themed shape, these classic raised images can add subtle dimension to backgrounds, photo mats and more. Once you've mastered simple dry embossing techniques, learn to change the face of designs by debossing or coloring images with chalks or paints for endless looks. (See pages 195-198.)

Step 1:
■ Place brass embossing (or other) template face up on a light box.

Step 2:
■ Position cardstock face down on top of the template. (Hint: If you'd like to emboss a darker shade of cardstock, look for a variety with a white core—it will allow the light to shine through.)

Step 3:
■ Rub your palm or a piece of wax paper over the cardstock. The "oils" will help the stylus travel more smoothly. (Hint: If you have trouble with the template or cardstock shifting, tack them to the light box with painter's tape.)

Step 4:
■ Use an embossing stylus to trace the outline of the shape. It is not necessary to "color in" the entire image with the stylus. (Hint: Use the largest ball tip that will fit the stencil. If the tip is too big, it won't hug detailed corners, but one that's too small may puncture the cardstock.) Emboss lightly, going over the line several times rather than pressing too hard and piercing your cardstock.

Supplies *Embossing template:* Lasting Impressions For Paper.

4 THINGS: by Darcee Wadduops
Supplies *Vellum:* Flair Designs; *Texture template:* Carolee's Creation; *Rub-ons:* Making Memories; *Twill:* Creek Bank Creations; *Stamping ink:* Stampin' Up!; *Dimensional adhesive:* Aleene's Paper Glaze, Duncan Enterprises; *Chalk:* Deluxe Designs; *Pen:* Gelly Roll, Sakura.

SWEETEST LITTLE PRINCESS KITTY: by Nicole Keller
Supplies *Textured cardstock:* Bazzill Basics Paper; *Rhinestones:* Westrim Crafts; *Transparency:* Hammermill; *Stars:* Nicole's own design; *Computer fonts:* Witched (title) and Raceway (journaling), downloaded from the Internet.

FRIEND: by Shelley Anderson
Supplies *Textured cardstock:* Bazzill Basics Paper; *Patterned paper:* KI Memories; *Letter stamps:* PSX Design; *Stamping ink:* StazOn, Tsukineko; *Date stamp:* Office Depot; *Slide mount:* Scraps Ahoy; *"Friend" accent, orange flower and pink circle:* KI Memories; *Large "f":* My Mind's Eye; *Ribbon:* C.M. Offray & Son, Making Memories and Li'l Davis Designs; *Staples:* Making Memories.

Debossing

Step 1:

Follow the steps for dry embossing, but place the cardstock face up over the embossing template. (Hint: Trace the template's shape carefully, since stray lines will be visible on the top of your design.) Instead of resulting in a raised design, you'll achieve one that's inset into the cardstock.

Supplies *Embossing template:* Lasting Impressions For Paper.

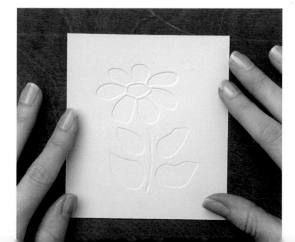

When you visit your grandparents, you and your cousins spend every possible moment in the water. Each year, grandma and grandpa add to the collection of water toys so you always have something new to play with. Even with all the new and exciting toys added to the mix, you all come back over and over again to the noodles. Some of the noodle games you play include noodle races, noodle wars, and the ever-popular noodle toss. You also love to see if you can balance on a noodle either in a sitting or standing position. As you get older and have had more practice, you balance for longer and longer periods of time. What doesn't seem to change is your fascination with these silly little pieces of foam. Gotta love a wet noodle!

Concentration +
Lots of arm movement =

balance

BALANCE: by Sue Thomas
Supplies *Textured cardstock:* Bazzill Basics Paper; *Embossing template:* ShapeBoss, Fiskars; *Lettering template:* Whimsical, Fiskars; *Pen:* VersaMark, Tsukineko; *Letter stickers:* Doodlebug Design; *Circle punch:* EK Success; *Computer fonts:* Arial Black and Garamond, Microsoft Word; *Other:* Corner rounder.

IDEA TO NOTE: After embossing the designs on her border strips, Sue traced them with a VersaMark pen to bring out the detailed designs.

SCHOOL PALS: by Miley Johnson
Supplies *Textured paper:* Bazzill Basics Paper;
Patterned papers: Autumn Leaves (circles) and Karen
Foster Design (notebook); *Chalk:* Close To My Heart;
Brads: Making Memories; *Letter stamps:* Stampers
Anonymous (title) and PSX Design (journaling);
Stamping ink: Stampin' Up!; *Other:* Clips and stencil.

TILLEY: by Nicole Keller
Supplies *Textured cardstock:* Bazzill Basics Paper;
Specialty paper: Provo Craft; *Template:* Lasting
Impressions for Paper; *Acrylic paint:* FolkArt, Plaid
Enterprises; *Stamping ink:* StazOn, Tsukineko; *Copper
sheeting:* Paragona; *Fibers:* DMC; *Computer font:* CK
Windsong, Becky Higgins' "Creative Clips and Fonts"
CD, *Creating Keepsakes.*

IDEA TO NOTE: Nicole used copper sheeting to create
her title and border strip.

Coloring embossed images

CHALK

Step 1:

■ Dry emboss using the steps outlined on page 192.

Step 2:

■ Flip the image over and use an applicator or cotton ball to give the raised design a subtle tint with chalk. For precision coloring, use a smaller applicator and a chalk eraser to remove stray chalk.

Supplies *Embossing template:* Lasting Impressions For Paper.

PAINT

Step 1:

■ Dry emboss using the steps outlined in this section.

Step 2:

■ Using acrylic paint and a small, dry brush, add random swatches of color to the raised design. (Hint: Avoid using too much paint to prevent warping.)

VARIATIONS • • • *Paint solid color over the entire surface or portions of the design, use watercolors to give the piece a subtle tint or carefully outline the image with watercolor pencils and use a blender or brush to pull color to the center. Add sparkle by painting with a thicker layer of acrylic paint and sprinkling with glitter or microbeads.*

Supplies *Embossing template:* Lasting Impressions For Paper.

SANDPAPER

Step 1:

■ Dry emboss using the steps outlined in this section using a white-core cardstock. (Hint: To be sure the cardstock has a white center, look along the paper's edge or make a small tear to check.)

Step 2:

■ Flip the image over. Using sandpaper or a wire brush, gently rub away the edges of the image to achieve a contrasting outline. (Hint: Don't press too hard, you'll flatten the image.)

Supplies *Embossing template:* Lasting Impressions For Paper.

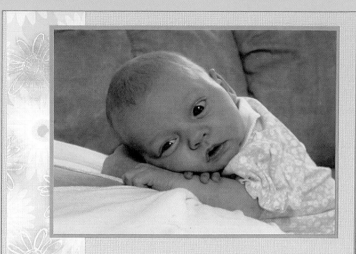

September 25, 2004... Today is the day you were due to be born. Instead, we were blessed with you 3 weeks early. Healthy, beautiful you. Thank you for becoming a part of our family. It has been a challenging 9 months, but it was worth it to have you here.

We ♥ you!

9 months later

9 MONTHS LATER: by Tracey Odachowski
Supplies *Textured cardstock:* Bazzill Basics Paper; *Patterned paper:* Chatterbox; *Stamping ink:* VersaMark, Tsukineko; *Embossing powder, pen, chalk and rubber stamps:* Stampin' Up!.

IDEA TO NOTE: Tracey rubbed chalk over the images on her border strip to add additional color and interest to her layout.

YOU ARE MY JOY: by Vanessa Hudson
Supplies *Patterned and embossed papers:* K & Company; *Butterfly accents:* K & Company; *Chalk:* Craf-T Products; *Foam stamps and acrylic paint:* Making Memories; *Small tag and paper hinges:* Vanessa's own designs; *Spray adhesive:* Krylon; *Other:* Ribbon and embroidery floss.

you are my

JOY

spring 2004

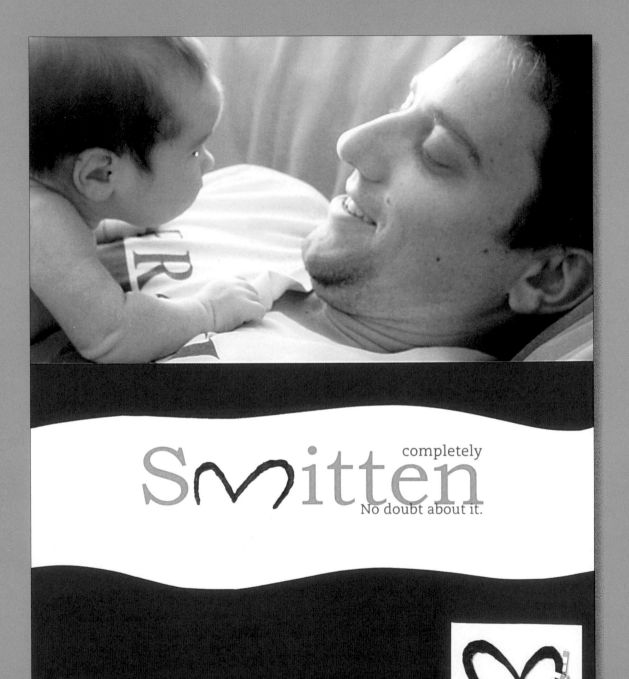

completely

Smitten

No doubt about it.

SMITTEN: by Shannon Montez
Supplies *Patterned paper:* Chatterbox; *Acrylic paint:* DecoArt; *Computer fonts:* Caecelia Roman and Bookman Old, downloaded from the Internet.

Miquelle
Age 7
Fall 2003

MIQUELLE: by Bonnie Lotz
Supplies *Patterned paper:* Provo Craft; *Lettering template:* College, ScrapPagerz.com; *Ribbon:* May Arts; *Embossing template:* Lasting Impressions for Paper; *Acrylic paint:* Delta Technical Coatings.

PINK, IT'S A GIRL THING: by Alisa Bangerter
Supplies *Embossing templates:* Mystical and Dragonflies, Fiskars; *Lettering template:* Whimsy, ScrapPagerz.com; *Embossing systems:* ShapeBoss and Mini ShapeBoss, Fiskars; *Texturing templates and tool:* Squares, Fiskars; *Flower template:* Fiskars; *Acrylic paint:* Delta Technical Coatings; *Buttons:* Making Memories; *Foam mounting squares:* Therm O Web; *Crochet thread:* DMC; *Computer font:* Monotype Corsiva, Microsoft Word.

IDEA TO NOTE: Alisa used a variety of embossing templates to create the raised look on her background paper and journaling box.

What is it about the color pink? Girls are attracted to it like butterflies are to the flowers. Sparkling pink lips, a myriad of charming pink bracelets, and flowery pink Capri pants are the perfect combination to make one feel so pretty. Off to fourth grade in such a fashion will hopefully make for an enchanting day. Pretty in pink. What more could a girl want?

PINK
...it's a girl thing.

THREE SISTERS: by Cindy Knowles
Supplies *Patterned paper:* K & Company; *Vellum:* EK Success; *Letter stamps:* Hero Arts; *Stamping ink:* StazOn, Tsukineko; *Metal letters:* Making Memories; *Fiber and T-pins:* EK Success; *Other:* Rickrack.

TREE SWING: by Natalie Call
Supplies *Patterned papers:* Rusty Pickle (red) and Karen Foster Design (blue); *Metal stencils:* Li'l Davis Designs; *Metal letters and ribbon:* Jo-Ann Stores; *Embossing templates:* American Traditional Designs (flower) and Lasting Impressions for Paper (dot); *Computer font:* CK Tall Type, Becky Higgins' "Creative Clips and Fonts" CD, *Creating Keepsakes.*

IDEA TO NOTE: Natalie used a combination of metal embellishments and metal stencil letters to create the embossed effects on her page.

Heat embossing

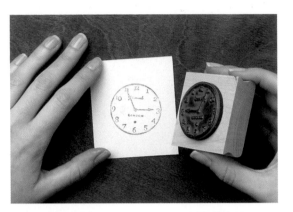

Gorgeous, dimensional designs are yours once you learn the simple tricks to heat embossing. With a little powder and a heat gun, stamped images, pre-made accents and even plain adhesives can go from "blah" to "bling" with professional-looking results. Add rich, shiny texture, change accent colors and even create faux tiles and glass with the following methods:

Step 1:

■ Stamp design with pigment, embossing or watermark ink (dye and solvent ink will dry too quickly). Use any color of ink, since it will be covered with embossing powder.

Step 2:

■ While ink is wet, sprinkle with embossing powder. (Hint: If powder is sticking to other sections of the cardstock, try rubbing the cardstock with a dryer sheet or a product specifically designed for embossing to reduce static.)

Step 3:

■ Direct hot air from a heat gun toward the surface, sweeping slowly back and forth, until the powder is completely melted. (Hint: To speed the process, place the item on mat board covered with aluminum foil to help it heat more quickly.)

Supplies *Stamp:* Rubber Stampede.

Ladybug

Ever since you were a baby, "ladybug" has been your nickname. Mostly we call you "Lexa-bug" using part real name and part nickname. It fits you perfectly. You are whimsical and colorful like a ladybug, and you never stay in one place for long. You dance from place to place. The best part is that you love the name. When you had a chance to have your face painted at Wheeler Farm, of course you chose a ladybug! 11/02

LADYBUG: by Natalie Call

Supplies *Letter stamps:* Ma Vinci's Reliquary; *Ladybug rubber stamp:* Stampcraft; *Embossing ink:* PSX Design; *Embossing powders:* Mark Enterprises; *Stamping ink:* Ranger Industries; *Sheet metal:* Making Memories.

IDEA TO NOTE: Natalie created the gold border strip on the bottom of her page by cutting a piece of blue cardstock, coating it with gold embossing powder and heat embossing it.

In the sweetness of **friendship** *let there be laughter & the sharing of pleasures.*
KAHLIL GIBRAN

Renee

Denise

Mary

Gina

JANUARY 2003

FRIENDSHIP: by Gina Sekelsky
Supplies *Patterned papers:* PSX Design (pink), K & Company (striped and green), KI Memories (green); *Rubber stamps:* Whipper Snapper Designs; *Stamping ink:* ColorBox, Clearsnap; *Embossing powder:* Ranger Industries; *Pen:* Zig Writer, EK Success; *Watercolors:* Derwent; *Other:* Raffia.

GRADUATION: by Kim Morgan
Supplies *Embossing powder:* Ranger Industries; *Tag, photo turns and rub-ons:* Making Memories; *Computer fonts:* Arial Narrow (journaling) and Pegsanna HMK, Microsoft Word.

IDEA TO NOTE: The "graduation" title and journaling strip is an interactive element that folds over the layout.

graduation

It's hard to describe the mix of feelings I experienced as I watched you cross that stage and receive your diploma. It was a thrill of pride, a sigh of relief, a surge of joy and a hint of sorrow all at the same time as I realized that this handsome, intelligent, confident young man was my firstborn son. And that now you are ready to begin stepping out to face the world and begin a life of your own. The Lord has blessed you with many talents. Use them well and you will always be blessed.
Love,
Mom

Creating lines and abstract patterns through heat embossing

Step 1:

■ Use roll-on embossing ink or an embossing pen to draw a freehand design, highlight edges or fashion an abstract border on cardstock.

Step 2:

■ While ink is wet, sprinkle with embossing powder.

Step 3:

■ Use a heat gun to melt the powder.

VARIATIONS • • • *Emboss without ink by sprinkling embossing powder over adhesive lines (like Therm O Web's Zips), adhesive dots, double-stick tape or glue stick, then melting with a heat gun.*

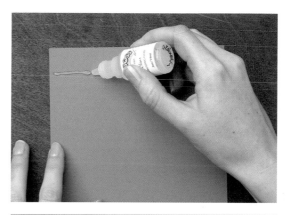

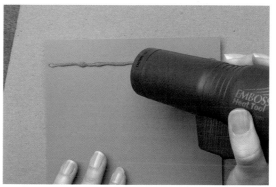

Impressing images with ultra thick embossing enamel

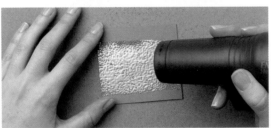

Step 1:
■ Coat the cardstock with watermark, embossing or pigment ink.

Step 2:
■ Sprinkle with Ultra Thick Embossing Enamel.

Step 3:
■ Direct hot air from a heat gun toward the surface, sweeping slowly back and forth, until powder is completely melted.

Step 4:
■ While the surface is still hot, sprinkle a second layer of UTEE across the top and melt with the heat gun. (Hint: If the powder doesn't stick, re-heat the surface with the embossing gun.) Repeat a third time and heat until the surface is completely smooth.

Step 5:
■ While the UTEE is hot, press a stamp—inked with watermark or embossing ink (or colored ink for added definition)—into the surface and hold until UTEE has cooled a bit. Remove stamp carefully.

Supplies *Stamp:* Stampa Rosa; *Ultra Thick Embossing Enamel:* Suze Weinberg.

slip

slide

splash

Ethan, Clara & Harrison ... Summer 2004

SLIP, SLIDE, SPLASH: by Kim Kesti
Supplies *Patterned paper and letter stickers:* KI Memories; *Tags:* American Tag Company; *Ribbon:* May Arts; *Stamping ink:* ColorBox, Clearsnap; *Embossing powder:* Hero Arts.

HEART BROKEN: by Linda Albrecht
Supplies *Patterned papers:* Chatterbox and Daisy D's Paper Paper Co.; *Paper letter stencils and stickers:* Chatterbox; *Ribbon:* Michaels; *Embossing powder:* Ranger Industries; *Embossing ink:* VersaMark, Tsukineko; *Transparency:* OfficeMax.

IDEA TO NOTE: Linda made her title by coating edges of stencil letters with ultra thick embossing enamel.

Creating "cracked glass"

Step 1:

■ Coat a photo, sticker or other accent with watermark or embossing ink.

Step 2:

■ Sprinkle with clear Ultra Thick Embossing Enamel.

Step 3:

■ Direct hot air from a heat gun toward the surface, sweeping slowly back and forth, until the powder is completely melted.

Step 4:

■ While the surface is still hot, sprinkle a second layer of UTEE across the top and melt with the heat gun. (Hint: If the powder doesn't stick, re-heat the surface with the embossing gun.) Repeat a third time and heat until surface is completely smooth.

Step 5:

■ Allow the UTEE to cool completely. Try placing it under a flat object in the freezer to speed the process and keep the piece from curling. After it has cooled, gently bend the piece to create several hairline cracks. (Hint: If any pieces of the UTEE begin to peel away from the surface, seal the accent with a clear glaze.)

Supplies *Sticker:* Art Warehouse, Creative Imaginations; *Ultra Thick Embossing Enamel:* Suze Weinberg.

SNOW PRINCESS: By Heather Preckel
Supplies *Textured cardstock:* Bazzill Basics Paper; *Tag:* Making Memories; *Ribbon:* Textured Trios, Michaels; *Button letters:* Junkitz; *Embossing enamel:* Suze Weinberg; *Rubber stamps:* Stampendous!; *Stamping ink:* Ranger Industries (brown); VersaMark, Tsukineko; *Pen:* Zig Writer, EK Success.

IDEA TO NOTE: To create the snowflake border on the top of her page, Heather stamped a white piece of cardstock. She rubbed a VersaMark watercolor stamp pad over the images, sprinkled them with a layer of ultra thick embossing enamel and melted the powder with a heat gun.

SWEET: by Miley Johnson
Supplies *Textured cardstock:* Bazzill Basics Paper; *Patterned paper:* Paperfever; *Stickers:* American Crafts; *Ribbon:* Memory Lane; *Beads:* Déjà Views, The C-Thru Ruler Company; *Computer font:* AL Capone, "Essential" CD, Autumn Leaves.

Creating custom color accents without ink

Step 1:

■ To change the color of a brad, grip the prong portion with tongs to prevent burning yourself.

Step 2:

■ Heat the brad top with an embossing gun.

Step 3:

■ Dip into regular embossing powder and remove. Use heat gun to completely melt powder until smooth. (Hint: If powder is not sticking to the brad top, heat it longer before dipping.) This process works with other metal accents as well.

VARIATIONS • • • *Add a metallic shine to mesh by trimming a piece, sprinkling regular embossing powder over the adhesive side, then heating with an embossing gun. Allow to cool, then use adhesives or fasteners to attach the mesh.*

Supplies *Brads:* Creative Imaginations; *Mesh:* Magic Mesh, Avant Card.

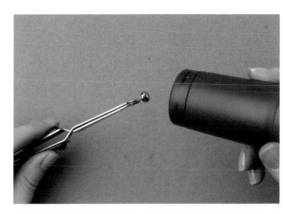

Transferring images

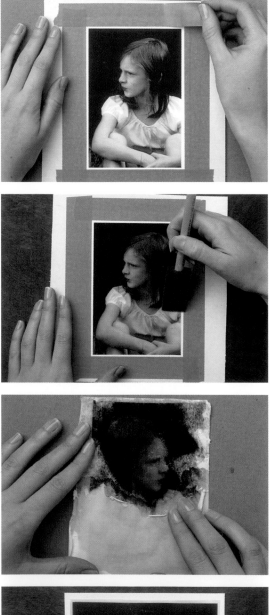

Turn photos into texturized works of art by transferring images to fabric, cardstock, tags, mica and more. Transfer techniques vary in the amount of time, effort and materials they require. Select a technique based on the image you have to transfer, the time you have available and the effect you'd like to achieve. Here are a few options:

WITH GEL MEDIUM

Step 1:
■ Using a toner-based image (not a regular photograph) in color or black and white, brush gel medium onto the front and allow to dry. (Hint: The gel medium will appear milky on the image, but will be clear when dry. Drying may take from two to four hours.)

Step 2:
■ After the first coat of gel medium is dry, brush on a second coat and allow to dry. Repeat this process until there are four or five coats of gel medium on the image.

Step 3:
■ After the gel medium has thoroughly dried, remove the image from surface and soak in water for approximately five minutes. (Hint: The gel medium will turn milky white during soaking, but will dry to a nearly transparent finish.)

Step 4:
■ Remove the image from water and peel or rub off the paper with your fingertips until it has been completely removed. (Hint: The completed image will be larger than the original size and resemble rolled polymer clay when handled.)

Step 5:
■ Allow the image to drip dry or smooth onto an absorbent cloth to dry. (Hint: Change the cloth one or two times during drying as water is absorbed from the transfer. Drying will take anywhere from six hours to overnight.)

Step 6:
■ Trim edges from the image and adhere to your layout or other project using a thin layer of gel medium or decoupage adhesive.

WITH GEL MEDIUM ONTO FABRIC

Step 1:

■ Choose the fabric appropriate for your project. Any light colored fabric or printer canvas will work well.

Step 2:

■ Scan a high-contrast color or black-and-white image and flip it horizontally so it will print onto your paper in a mirror-image of your final desired image. Change print setting to "high quality" or "fine" and print the image. (Hint: This technique will not work with a toner photocopy.)

Step 3:

■ Trim the picture leaving only a little white around the edge. Using a brush, apply a light coat of gel medium to the fabric.

Step 4:

■ Lay paper image face down onto the gel medium and use fingers to smooth out any air bubbles.

Step 5:

■ Burnish paper image with a brayer, the back of a spoon, a bone folder or similar tool for about 10-15 seconds. Lift corner to check on the transfer progress and burnish again if necessary.

Step 6:

■ Peel paper image from the fabric. (Hint: If the paper was left on too long, let the transfer dry completely, then use a little water on your finger tip to rub off excess paper.)

WITH XYLENE BLENDER PEN

Step 1:

■ Using a toner-based photocopier, copy an image in color or black and white. (Hint: It will be necessary to have the image flipped horizontally when copied.)

Step 2:

■ Place the image face down onto the background and tape in place with low-tack tape to keep it still while transferring.

Step 3:

■ Using a Xylene-based blender pen, "color" over the image in sections to soak. (Hint: Work in a well-ventilated area since the pen will emit strong fumes.)

Step 4:

■ Burnish each section with the back of a spoon, bone folder or similar tool. Lift the corner every so often to check the progress of the transfer. (Hint: If transfer is not quite complete, soak and burnish a little more.)

Step 5:

■ After the ink has transferred, remove the paper.

WITH PACKING TAPE

Step 1:

■ Attach a strip of packing tape to the front of a toner photocopy or glossy magazine image.

Step 2:

■ Burnish using the back of a spoon, a brayer, a bone folder or similar tool.

Step 3:

■ Soak the image in water for approximately five minutes. Rub the paper from the tape under running water.

Step 4:

■ The completed packing tape transfer will remain tacky after drying. Adhere finished product to your project surface.

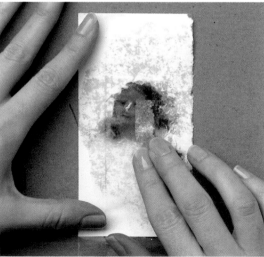

LAUGH, GIGGLE, FUNNY, SILLY: by Christy Tomlinson
Supplies *Textured cardstock:* Bazzill Basics Paper; *Patterned paper:* Chatterbox; *Ribbon:* May Arts and Making Memories; *Safety pins:* Making Memories; *Stamping ink:* Distressed Ink, Ranger Industries; *Clip art:* "Heritage, Vintage & Retro Collection" CD, *Creating Keepsakes.*

IDEA TO NOTE: Christy used image transfer to transfer the small photograph of her children to the charm featured on her page.

KATIE AND LEAH: by Kelly Latenbach
Supplies *Textured cardstock:* Bazzill Basics Paper; *Rubber stamp:* Stampers Anonymous; *Stamping ink:* StazOn, Tsukineko; *Computer fonts:* 2Peas Price Check, 2Peas Sonnet Script, 2Peas Style Magnet, downloaded from *www.two-peasinabucket.com*; AL Scratched, "Vintage" CD; AL Professor, "Handwritten" CD; AL Charisma, "Script" CD; AL Highlight, "Essential" CD, Autumn Leaves; CBX-Chippy Circles, Journaling Font CD, Chatterbox; Steelfish, downloaded from the Internet.

IDEA TO NOTE: Notice how Kelly used a packing tape transfer with her photograph and the frame that surrounds it.

YOU ARE LOVED: by Vanessa Hudson
Supplies *Textured cardstock:* Bazzill Basics Paper; *Patterned paper:* K & Company; *Metal frame, hinges, brads and stickers:* K & Company; *Stamping ink:* Ranger Industries; *Photo transfer pen:* Xylene; *Other:* Ribbon.

IDEA TO NOTE: To create the old-fashioned look on the picture in the middle of her layout, Vanessa used a xylene pen to transfer a photo of herself and her daughter to Bazzill cardstock.

GIGGLE TIL IT HURTS: by Shelley Anderson
Supplies *Patterned paper:* Chatterbox; *Rub-ons, buttons, brads, bookplate, string, date stamp and silver eyelet:* Making Memories; *Label maker:* Dymo; *Photo turns:* 7gypsies; *Bubble letters:* Li'l Davis Designs; *Stamping ink:* StazOn, Tsukineko; *Image transfer pen:* Eberhard Faber; *Antique brads:* Boxer Scrapbook Productions.

HOW TO   Using metal stamps

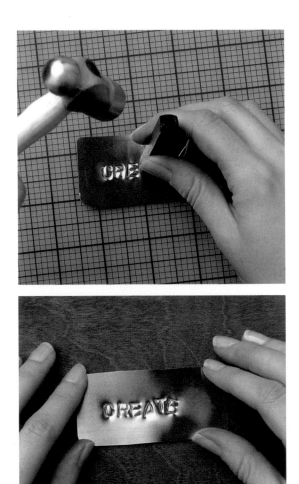

Who knew that a simple whack of a hammer could produce such professional results? With a few taps, metal stamps can etch custom text and designs into metal sheeting, plain dog tags, leather, damp clay and other materials. It's much easier—and more impressive—than you'd think.

Step 1:
■ Place a metal sheet on a flat surface (some scrapbookers prefer a self-healing mat, while others stamp on a hard surface).

Step 2:
■ Position a metal stamp where desired, and hit the back firmly with a hammer. If the letter is not completely set, simply reposition the stamp and hammer again. (Hint: To place stamps exactly where you'd like them, position them at eye level. The images will reflect in the metal, allowing you to see exactly where they'll fall.)

Supplies *Metal stamps and metal sheet:* Making Memories.

FATHER'S DAY: by Marilyn Healey
Supplies *Textured cardstock:* Provo Craft; *Specialty paper:* Creative Imaginations; *Metal sheets and stamps:* Making Memories; *Stamping ink:* Nick Bantock, Ranger Industries; *Letter rub-ons:* Li'l Davis Designs; *"F" index card:* Autumn Leaves; *Embroidery floss:* DMC; *Other:* Silver heart and eyelets.

LUCKY ME: by Cindy Knowles
Supplies *Patterned paper:* Daisy D's Paper Paper Co.; *Metal stamps:* Source unknown; *Fiber scraps:* E-Z Walnut Ink; *Stamping ink:* StazOn, Tsukineko; *Metal tag:* Boxer Scrapbook Productions; *Computer font:* Stamper Face, downloaded from the Internet; *Other:* Paper clips, brad, rubber bands, leather, cork and metal.

IDEA TO NOTE: Cindy used metal stamps on a variety of materials on this layout: leather, paper, metal, cork and her photograph.

Adding metallic touches

Want to add eye-catching glitz to your layouts but don't want the weight of bulky metallic accents? Whether you're aiming for a glamorous formal finish or funky industrial look, produce a little shimmer with metallic paint, markers, beads, rub-ons or one of these simple techniques:

WITH FOIL

Step 1:
■ Trace over or freehand a design with liquid adhesive. Allow to dry until tacky.

Step 2:
■ Place a foil sheet over the image and press firmly onto the glued areas.

Step 3:
■ Peel sheet back gently. If foil is not adhered to the design, press again or reapply glue to that area before trying again. (Hint: This technique also works with a thin layer of glue over stamped images, computer-printed titles, pre-made accents, die cuts, stickers and punches.)

VARIATIONS • • • *Apply fine lines or create detailed designs onto cardstock by "writing" over the foil sheets with a battery-operated Hot Foil Pen (available from Staedtler). Print an image on vellum or thin paper, lay it on top of the foil and trace it slowly with the pen to transfer the foiled image to your background.*

Supplies *Foil:* Staedtler.

WITH LEAF FLAKE

Step 1:
■ To create a pattern, place double-stick tape where you'd like the flakes to appear.

Step 2:
■ Press loose leaf flakes onto the adhesive. (Hint: Work over scrap paper; excess flakes will fly out in several directions!)

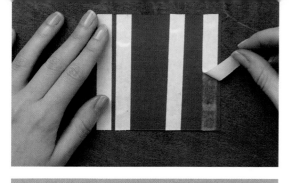

WITH LEAFING PENS

Step 1:

■ Prime the pen according to package instructions.

Step 2:

■ Add highlights to pre-made accents, die cuts and more by dragging or dabbing metallic ink along edges or image highlights. Allow to dry completely.

VARIATIONS • • • *Use the pen to write custom titles and journaling or to re-color metal or acrylic accents. Create custom backgrounds by dabbing ink onto glossy paper, then spritzing with water or covering with wax paper and rolling over it with a brayer before removing.*

Supplies *Leafing pen:* Krylon; *Punch out:* KI Memories.

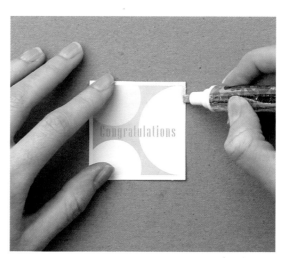

Step 3:

■ Use a stiff brush to wipe away excess flakes, then flip the piece over and burnish to set.

VARIATIONS • • • *Customize pre-made accents with leaf flake by applying liquid adhesive to desired spots, allowing to dry until tacky, then pressing flakes on. Use this technique to adorn punches, die cuts and other cardstock accents with glitter and microbeads as well.*

Supplies *Leaf flake:* Magic Scraps.

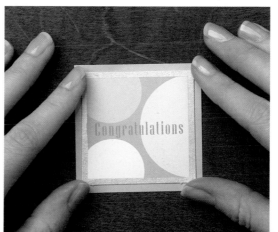

WITH GLITTER

Step 1:

■ Spread a thin layer of liquid adhesive or double-stick tape over the surface of your design.

Step 2:

■ Place the piece over scrap paper or a shallow pan and sprinkle liberally with glitter. Tap off any excess. After a few minutes, flip the piece over and burnish to "set" the glitter. (Hint: You can also coat the piece with a clear glaze to completely seal the flakes.)

VARIATIONS • • • *Apply glue in squiggles or only to the outline or highlights of an image for a variety of looks. Achieve two-tone effects by applying glue to one section, adding glitter, then applying glue to the remainder before sprinkling with a contrasting color. Glitter can also be used to glitz up brads, eyelets, tiles or acrylic accents—simply coat the top with glue, dip into glitter and allow to dry completely.*

BEAUTY: by Laurie Stamas
Supplies *Textured cardstock:* Bazzill Basics Paper; *Patterned paper:* Rhonna Farrer Collection, Autumn Leaves; *Rub-ons:* Autumn Leaves; *Metal frame, chipboard letters and acrylic paint:* Making Memories; *Metal letters:* Pressed Petals; *Quote:* KI Memories; *Ribbon charm:* Maya Road; *Other:* Engraved jewelry ring and silk ribbon.

IDEA TO NOTE: Laurie says, "metallic pens are great for mimicking the look of a metallic accent on your page, without adding any extra weight. For this layout, I used a leafing pen to mat the edge of my photo and the edge of my quote. I also used it to make my chipboard letters look metallic because I wanted them to coordinate with the other metal accents on my page."

dream (drem) 1. vis... during sleep 2. the desire...

created by ones subconscious mind ...eat 3. a fond hope

When she wore Great-Grandma's fur hat and collar, she dreamed of tea and crumpets, a life of luxury, and long train trips through far away lands . . .

A
B
C
D

DREAM: by Sharon Lewis
Supplies *Textured cardstock:* Bazzill Basics Paper; *Patterned paper, definition sticker, eyelet and brads:* Making Memories; *Leaf flake:* Leaf Tek; *Stamping ink:* ColorBox, Clearsnap; *Other:* Ribbon.

WONDERFUL ONE: by Marilyn Healey
Supplies *Patterned paper and accents:* KI Memories; *Glitter and die cut:* Provo Craft; *Paper ribbon:* Twistel, Making Memories; *Tag:* Avery; *Computer font:* LD Delightful, Package unknown, Inspire Graphics; *Other:* Ribbon.

BUTTERFLY: by Nely Fok
Supplies *Patterned paper:* K & Company; *Ribbon:* Making Memories; *Transparency:* Hammermill; *Glitter:* Art Institute; *Rubber stamp:* The Stamping Bug; *Stamping ink:* Adirondack, Ranger Industries; Brilliance, Tsukineko; *Computer font:* 2Peas Gingersnap, downloaded from *www.twopeasinabucket.com*; *Other:* Paper flowers.

IDEA TO NOTE: Nely created her butterfly accent by stamping a butterfly image on a transparency and cutting it out. She wiped the transparency with rubbing alcohol to remove static from the transparency and carefully glued glitter on the back of the butterfly image.

Using mica

It's remarkable when something that seems so fragile can be so strong. Translucent mica pieces can be peeled apart to impossibly thin layers that are still durable enough to withstand heat embossing, stamping, image transfer and more. Experiment with techniques that also include layering, pressing and coloring—you'll be thrilled with what this material can do.

Step 1:

■ Wedge a sharp object, such as a paper piercer, between the edges of your mica sheet to separate the layers. Peel carefully, bearing in mind that thinner layers may crack during the process. Stop peeling when the mica reaches the desired shade or thickness.

Step 2:

■ Coat one side completely with a clear-drying adhesive and press onto a photo, pre-made accent or other embellishments as a glass-like top layer. (Hint: Adhering over a slightly dimensional object may cause small air pockets in the adhesive.)

VARIATIONS • • • *Mica can also be cut with scissors, edged with a leafing pen or punched. When stamping, heat embossing or transferring images to mica, proceed as you would with other slick surfaces, such as vellum or transparencies.*

Supplies *Mica:* USArtquest; *Flowers:* Colorbok.

OH THE PLACES YOU'LL GO: by Joanna Bolick

Supplies *Patterned paper:* Mustard Moon; *Mica:* USArtQuest; *Transparency:* Office Depot; *Computer fonts:* Adobe Caslon Pro, Adobe Creative Suite; Donata and Century, downloaded from the Internet.

IDEA TO NOTE: To create the circular mica accents on her page, Joanna printed text on a transparency, cut it out, and adhered it to the mica with diamond glaze.

Using paint

Watercolors, acrylics, metallics and more...paint may be the quintessential coloring tool for creating custom accents and changing the face of existing ones. From a quick dry brushing to more complicated texturizing techniques, paints can supply the color, dimension, and pizzazz that can dramatically impact your layouts. Experiment with these techniques:

ACRYLIC, DRY BRUSHING

Step 1:
■ Dip a stiff-bristled brush into acrylic paint.

Step 2:
■ Pounce bristles on a piece of scrap paper until the brush is barely holding any paint.

Step 3:
■ Brush in long strokes across your paper or cardstock. Brush a second time in a perpendicular motion for a crosshatch pattern.

ACRYLIC, WITH CRACKLE MEDIUM

Step 1:
■ Brush a thick coat of acrylic paint onto thick cardstock or chipboard. Allow to dry completely.

Step 2:
■ Brush on a medium coat of crackle medium. Allow to dry until just tacky.

Step 3:
■ Brush on a thin coat of a contrasting color of acrylic paint. Top layer will crack as it dries, revealing the original coat of paint beneath.

VARIATIONS • • • *The direction of your brushstrokes when applying the top layer of paint will determine the appearance of the cracks. Long brushstrokes will result in mostly straight cracks, strokes perpendicular to one another will produce a crosshatch of cracks, while small or swirling strokes will give you a surface of hairline cracks.*

TROUBLE TROUBLE TROUBLE TROUBLE TROUBLE TROUBLE TR

Every once in a while you give me this look...it isn't really naughty...well occasionally it is...but most of the time it is just SMUG!

You are so sure of yourself. I want to tell you to slow down, be a baby a little longer, but you are off and running...and climbing...and jumping...and learning...and giving me this look.

The "don't worry mom" look. I know I will see it many times, but I wasn't expecting to see it so soon. To be honest it scares me a little...if you think you can do it all without me at 17 months old what will you be like at 17 years old?

You will probably still be "trouble" and able to melt my heart with a single look...even if its a look that tells me that I have no idea what I am in for...but you do!

The LOOK

ConFIdenCe iS bEautIfUL

May 04

THE LOOK: by Lisa Damrosch
Supplies *Patterned papers:* Rusty Pickle (black and yellow stripe), 7gypsies (red), Daisy D's Paper Co. (sand) and Chatterbox (grey); *Brads, photo turns, ribbon and safety pins:* Making Memories; *Label tape:* Dymo; *Stamping ink:* Ranger Industries; *Pen:* Zig Millennium, EK Success; *Letter stencil and twill phrase:* Li'l Davis Designs; *Rub-ons:* Autumn Leaves; *Computer font:* 2Peas Renaissance, downloaded from *www.twopeasinabucket.com*; *Other:* Acrylic paint and transparency.

Painting metal

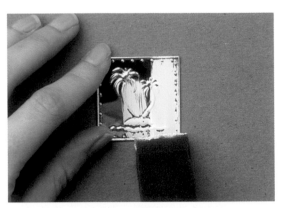

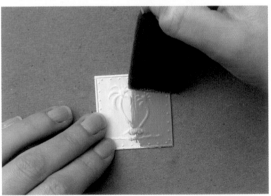

ACRYLIC, PAINTING METAL

Step 1:

■ Change the color of metal accents by first coating with a layer or two of gesso (to prime the surface to help the paint adhere) if desired.

Step 2:

■ Apply one to two coats of paint and allow to dry completely. (Hint: For a glossy finish, add a top coat of glaze to the piece.)

Step 3:

■ For an aged look, apply a medium-thick coat of paint and sand a bit before it's completely dry. (Hint: You can also paint directly on the metal, leaving off the gesso, which will allow the dried paint to be sanded or scratched easily.)

VARIATIONS • • • *Apply a coat of paint to metal accents with recessed images, then use a wet paper towel to wipe away the paint. The color will remain in the design, adding visual punch.*

Supplies *Metal tile:* Scrapyard 329.

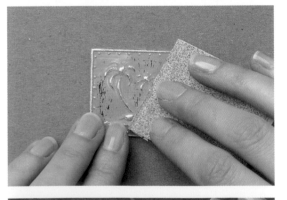

M: by Miley Johnson
Supplies *Patterned paper*: Chatterbox; *Metal phrases, molding strips and acrylic paint*: Making Memories; *Flower accent*: Hobby Lobby; *Other*: Wood letter.

Creating texture

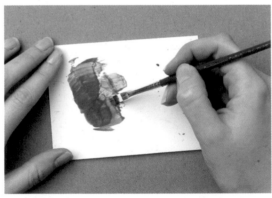

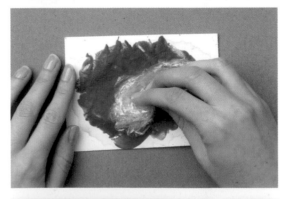

ACRYLIC, TEXTURIZING

Step 1:

■ Mix acrylic paint with gel medium until the desired consistency is achieved. (Hint: The more paint, the thinner the texture.)

Step 2:

■ Apply a thick layer to heavy cardstock or chipboard.

Step 3:

■ Add more texture by gently dabbing with a wad of cellophane or by building ridges with a palette knife.

VARIATIONS • • • *Create interesting patterns by dragging a painter's comb or fork across the surface or by pressing stamps or textured items into the paint.*

ACRYLIC, FAUX TEXTURE

Step 1:

■ Achieve easy texture by pressing a layer of mesh onto cardstock. (Hint: Be sure it's completely adhered to prevent paint from seeping below the mesh.)

Step 2:

■ Dip a dry brush into acrylic paint and pounce the bristles on a piece of scrap paper until they're barely holding any paint.

Step 3:

■ Sweep the brush back and forth across the mesh until the cardstock appears to be covered with a light layer of paint.

Step 4:

■ Allow to dry for a few minutes, then peel back the mesh.

VARIATIONS • • • *Try painting over lace, metal screening or any other "open" materials. Paint can also be applied over stencils and templates, as well.*

Supplies *Mesh:* Sonnets, Creative Imaginations.

ACRYLIC, SPONGING/STIPPLING

Step 1:
■ Create a mottled look by dipping a sea sponge or stippling brush into acrylic paint.

Step 2:
■ Apply in pouncing motion to cardstock until the desired look is achieved.

Step 3:
■ For visual interest, repeat the process with a second and third color of paint, allowing colors to overlap and build up texture.

Watercolor washing

Step 1:
Heat emboss an image following the technique outlined in the section on "heat embossing" on page 204. Use a shade of embossing powder that matches the background.

Step 2:
Load a wet paintbrush with color and swirl over the surface. The embossed image will "resist" the paint, resulting in a faux bleached finish.

Step 3:
Paint the entire surface, building up color until you achieve the desired shading.

SPRING GIRLS: by Natalie Call

Supplies *Patterned papers:* BasicGrey (pink and orange), Making Memories (green); *Foam stamps:* Michael's Craft store; *Embossing ink:* PSX Design; *Embossing powder:* Stampin' Up!; *Embossing pen:* Zig Writer, EK Success; *Watercolors:* ArtAdvantage; *Word charm:* Doodlebug Designs; *Fiber:* Pebbles Inc.; *Computer font:* CK Sloppy, "Creative Clips and Fonts" CD, *Creating Keepsakes*.

IDEA TO NOTE: To create the embossed accents on her page, Natalie stamped and embossed the flower images. She then did a watercolor wash over the top of the flowers to bring out the details in the stamp.

Using watercolor pencils

Step 1:
■ Color, outline or highlight an image with watercolor pencils just as you would with regular colored pencils.

Step 2:
■ Using a wet paintbrush or blender pen, pull color toward the center to achieve soft color washes or bold highlights.

KATIE AND LAYNE: by Kelly Lautenbach
Supplies *Textured cardstock:* Bazzill Basics Paper; *Watercolor pencils:* General; *Water pen:* Close To My Heart; *Brads:* Lasting Impressions for Paper; *Pen:* Zig Writer, EK Success; *Ribbon:* May Arts.

OUR BUNDLE OF JOY: by Gina Sekelsky
Supplies *Watercolor pencils:* Derwent; *Glitter glue:* PSX Design; *Pen:* EK Success; *Leaf accents:* Gina's own design; *Thread:* YLI.

IDEA TO NOTE: Gina freehand painted the illustration on her page, using a combination of watercolor pencils, a Tombow blender pen and a wet paintbrush.

Using pigment powders

Like the sweep of eye shadow over a lid, a little pigment powder can supply a lot of color, sparkle and glamour. Blend it with mediums or paints to design your own shimmering custom colors, or brush it over inks for a light, luminous finish. Whoever thought dusting could be so much fun?

MIXING WITH MEDIUMS

Step 1:
■ Mix a bit of powder into gum arabic or gel medium until well blended.

Step 2:
■ Use it to paint freehand designs or add highlights to pre-made accents, embellishments or collage projects.

VARIATIONS • • • *Mix powder into acrylic paint, modeling paste and more to create a lustrous finish.*

Supplies *Pigment powder:* PearlX, Jacquard Products.

BRUSHING OVER INK

Step 1:
■ Stamp image with watermark, embossing or pigment ink.

Step 2:
■ While ink is still sticky, use a paintbrush to dust the surface with powder, then use a tissue or brush to wipe away excess powder.

VARIATIONS • • • *Try dipping a blender pen into pigment powder and "painting" with it. The blender will "set" the powder.*

Supplies *Pigment powder:* Perfect Pearls; *Stamp:* Making Memories.

GREATER AND LONGER CHILDHOOD:
by Tracey Odachowski
Supplies *Patterned paper, rubber stamp and sticker:* Club Scrap; *Stamping ink:* VersaMark, Tsukineko; *Embossing powder and pen:* Stampin' Up!; *Pigment powder:* Pearl-Ex, Jacquard Products.

IDEA TO NOTE: Tracy created her border by stamping a ticket stamp onto cardstock. She embossed the images and brushed the cooled images with Pearl Ex.

BECOMING PIRATES: by Julie Scattaregia
Supplies *Patterned paper:* BasicGrey; *Pigment powder:* Pearl-Ex, Jacquard Products; *Stamping ink:* VersaMark, Tsukineko; *Foam stamps:* Li'l Davis Designs (P, I and T) and Making Memories (R, A, E and S); *Date rub-ons, bubble letters and metal frames:* Li'l Davis Designs; *Rub-ons and red frame:* Making Memories; *Photo turns:* 7gypsies; *Ribbon:* C.M. Offray & Son; *Rubber stamps:* EK Success; *Label maker:* Dymo; *Other:* Fabric.

IDEA TO NOTE: Julie created the title on her page by inking foam stamps with a VersaMark pad. She then applied Pearl Ex to the images with a brush and sealed the images with clear embossing powder.

Using polymer clay

Roll it, stamp it, form it, press it. Whatever technique you'd like to try, clay is a receptive surface. But don't be fooled. Though it's a visual heavyweight, clay is surprisingly light and can be rolled paper thin so you don't add bulk to your pages. Give it a try with one of these ideas:

STAMPING

Step 1:

■ Knead clay until it's easily workable. Roll to desired thickness.

Step 2:

■ Press stamp gently into the clay. Remove carefully. Use scissors or a craft knife to trim to desired size. (Hint: Bold-image stamps work best. If stamp is sticking, try coating it with watermark ink or colored ink for added definition.)

Step 3:

■ Dry clay according to package instructions. Many brands require oven baking, while others can be left to air dry overnight.

Step 4:

■ Use "as is," coat with a layer of glaze or color with paint, chalk or metallic rub-ons.

VARIATIONS • • • *Press dimensional items or fabric into the clay to add texture. White clay can also be colored by mixing in a bit of acrylic paint before rolling.*

Supplies *Stamp:* Rubber Stampede; *Clay:* Makins Clay, Provo Craft.

The giraffe exhibit at Binder Park is an amazing experience. A bridge is built at "head level" with the giraffes so that guests can pet them and feed them biscuits. I've loved giraffes since I was a very little girl, and I have to say having the chance to meet and pet one literally one face to face was an experience I'll never forget.

Binder Park Zoo

BINDER PARK ZOO: by Heidi Stepanova
Supplies *Patterned and textured papers:* Club Scrap; *Metallic paper:* Provo Craft; *Handmade paper:* Source unknown; *Rubber stamp:* Embossing Arts; *Clay:* Pr?mo, Sculpey; *Stamping ink:* ColorBox, Clearsnap; *Bookplate and photo turns:* Making Memories; *Fibers:* Fiber Scraps; *Computer font:* Times New Roman, Microsoft Word.

IDEA TO NOTE: Heidi stamped her image into paper clay with gold ink to create a dimensional accent that fits the theme of her page.

Making accents with polymer clay

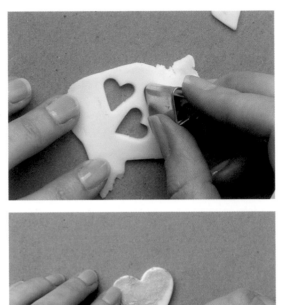

Step 1:
■ Knead clay until it's easily workable. Roll to desired thickness.

Step 2:
■ Cut with small cookie cutters, decorative rotary blades or a craft knife and alphabet or shape templates. Use a paper piercer to make a hole if you'd like to "hang" your finished accent.

Step 3:
■ To add interest, paint the dried accent, allow to dry, then stamp with solvent ink. Add a coat of glaze for shine.

Step 4:
■ Copy step 3 from p. 242

VARIATIONS • • • *Clay can also be pressed into molds or sculpted into unique designs.*

Supplies *Clay and cutters:* Makins Clay, Provo Craft; *Stamp:* Making Memories; *Stamping ink:* StazOn, Tsukineko.

MUSEUM OF ANCIENT LIFE: by Diane Garding
Supplies *Patterned paper and brads:* Provo Craft; *Computer font:* PC Rat-a-Tat, "A Gathering of Friends" CD, Provo Craft; *Polymer clay:* Sculpey; *Iron-on transfer paper:* Ink Jet; *Logo:* downloaded from the Internet.

IDEA TO NOTE: Diane created her own dinosaur tile accents by downloading images from the Internet, transferring them to paper clay and baking them in the oven.

Using rubber stamps

As the rubber stamping and scrapbooking worlds begin to blend into one, you'll find more stamped images sneaking onto layouts. And though basic designs still use traditional dye or pigment inks, stamped images and alphabets are now appearing on diverse materials as new inks and techniques emerge. Here's a sample of some simple stamping looks:

WITH INK

Step 1:

■ Hold stamp, rubber side up, in the palm of one hand. Tap an inkpad onto the surface until the entire image is covered.

Step 2:

■ If using dye ink, breathe hot air on the stamp (as you would if cleaning a pair of glasses) to "freshen" the ink. Press firmly onto the surface without rocking back and forth. Lift and allow to dry completely.

VARIATIONS • • • *To place stamp in an exact position, use a stamp positioner. Stamp the image onto a piece of transparency, position it in the desired spot, line the stamp positioner up with the image, remove the transparency and place the inked stamp into the corner of the positioner before pressing.*

Supplies *Stamp:* Stampa Rosa.

TEN: by Joy Bohon

Supplies *Patterned paper and bookplates:* Creative Imaginations; *Transparency:* Narratives, Creative Imaginations; *Rubber Stamps:* Limited Edition Rubberstamps, FontWerks, MOBE and Ma Vinci's Reliquary; *Stamping ink:* VersaColor and StazOn, Tsukineko; *Tags:* Making Memories; *Clips and bar:* 7gypsies; *Brads:* Lost Art Treasures; *Wooden letters:* Li'l Davis Designs; *Computer font:* Casablanca Antique, downloaded from the Internet.

Stamping with acrylic paint

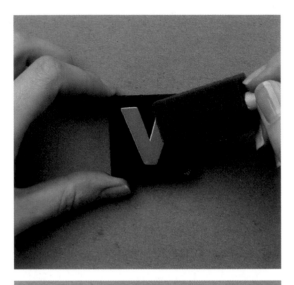

Step 1:
■ Use a paintbrush to cover the stamp—foam stamps work best—with a light coat of acrylic paint. (Hint: Stamp on scrap paper first to determine how much paint will result in a crisp image.)

Step 2:
■ Press carefully onto the cardstock to prevent stamp from sliding. Remove and allow to dry completely.

VARIATION • • • *For a shabbier look, dip the stamp directly into paint and press onto cardstock. Or add more color by painting on additional shades or designs before stamping.*

Supplies *Foam alphabet stamps:* Michaels.

Floating Fun: by Jenny Jackson
Supplies *Patterned paper:* Scrapworks; *Letter stickers:* KI Memories; *Tiles:* Junkitz; *Brads:* Scrapworks; *Ribbon:* May Arts and C.M. Offray & Son; *Letter stamps and acrylic paint:* Making Memories.

Stamping with bleach

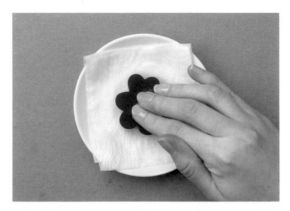

Step 1:
■ Line a shallow dish with a few layers of paper towels. Saturate the towels with bleach.

Step 2:
■ Press a stamp into the bleach and press onto cardstock. (Hint: Bold image stamps work best, as do darker shades of cardstock.)

Step 3:
■ Allow to dry completely. Experiment with a variety of cardstock colors and manufacturers—each will produce a different effect!

Supplies *Stamp:* Suzie's Zoo.

THE GIRL'S GOT STYLE – NOT: by Shannon Taylor
Supplies *Patterned paper:* BasicGrey; *Rubber stamp:* Paper Candy; *Buckle:* Rusty Pickle; *Transparency:* Magic Scraps; *Nail heads:* Scrapworks; *Ribbon:* C.M. Offray & Son; *Letter stamps:* Hero Arts and Stampin' Up! ("O"); *Jump rings:* Junkitz; *Dimensional adhesive:* Diamond Glaze, JudiKins; *Computer fonts:* Misfit (title) and Pitch, downloaded from the Internet; *Adhesive:* Super Tape, Therm O Web.

Stamping with solvent ink

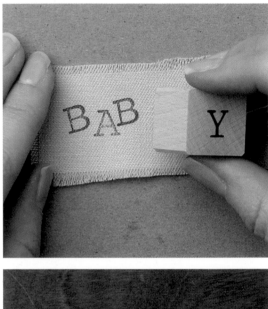

Step 1:

■ Add designs to fabric, ribbon and more by coating stamp with solvent ink and gently pressing onto the material. (Hint: Test on a scrap first to determine the amount of ink and pressure to use to prevent the image from bleeding.)

Step 2:

■ Add definition to edges or give fabric a shabby touch by lightly brushing ink across the surface.

VARIATION • • • *Add stamped images to slick surfaces, such as transparencies, vellum, metal, mica or glass microscope slides, with solvent ink. Press stamp carefully to keep image from "sliding."*

Supplies *Alphabet stamps:* PSX Design; *Stamping ink:* StazOn, Tsukineko.

Suddenly Nina cares about clothes. She says her Old Navy hat makes her look cool. When will she learn that combed hair is cool, too?

fashionista

FASHIONISTA: by Elizabeth Russka
Supplies *Textured cardstock:* Bazzill Basics Paper; *Patterned paper:* KI Memories; *Fabric:* Cath Kidston (floral); Swatches, Junkitz (twill); *Letter stamps:* PSX Design; *Rubber stamps:* Ma Vinci's Reliquary; *Staples:* Making Memories; *Stamping ink:* StazOn, Tsukineko; *Other:* Buckle.

Stamping with watermark ink

Step 1:

■ Add a subtle design to cardstock by pressing a stamp inked with watermark ink onto the surface.

Step 2:

■ For a suede-like finish, brush the surface with chalk. The rich color will adhere to the stamped image and give a soft tint to the background.

VARIATION • • • *Brush ink with pigment powder instead for a shimmering finish.*

Supplies *Stamp:* Making Memories; *Stamping ink:* VersaMark, Tsukineko.

THE GRADUATE: by Maya Opavska
Supplies *Textured cardstock:* Bazzill Basics Paper; *Patterned paper and border sticker:* Sweetwater; *Foam stamps and acrylic paint:* Making Memories; *Square punch:* Marvy Uchida; *Rubber stamps:* Stampin' Up! (sunflowers), Turtle Press ("2004"), River City Rubber Works ("spring"); *Stamping ink:* Tsukineko; *Ribbon:* Li'l Davis Designs; *Chalk:* Stampin' Up!; *Pen:* Fabrico, Tsukineko; *Computer font:* CK Artisan, Becky Higgins' "Creative Clips & Fonts" CD, *Creating Keepsakes;* *Other:* Thread and fiber.

Masking while stamping

Step 1:
■ Stamp an image onto scrap paper and trim with scissors.

Step 2:
■ Stamp the same image onto cardstock in the desired position.

Step 3:
■ Tack the trimmed mask over the real image with removable adhesive.

Step 4:
■ Press a second stamp onto the surface. Remove the mask. The process will result in multiple images that do not overlap.

GABRIEL'S FIRST HALLOWEEN: by Bonnie Lotz
Supplies *Letter stamps:* PSX Design (small) and Ma Vinci's Reliquary (large); *Ribbon:* May Arts; *Rubber stamps:* Rubber Stampede; *Eyelets:* Making Memories; *Other:* Twill.

Machine stitching

Stitching (either with a machine or by hand) is an ideal way to add a hint of texture and detail to your layouts. Sew to connect two items or use it as a purely decorative element. Either way, you've found the perfect finishing touch.

WITH MACHINE

Step 1:

■ Adhere the material to be sewn to the background to prevent shifting. (Hint: For sheer items like vellum, use clips or your spare hand to hold it in place.)

Step 2:

■ Select the stitch length, style and tension on your machine and slowly feed the materials through. (Hint: To sew through cardstock, try using heavy-duty needles—such as those for denim—and use longer stitches to avoid simply perforating your cardstock.)

E-ELLA: by Hilary Shirley
Supplies *Patterned papers:* Bo-Bunny Press (red and white floral), Making Memories (polka dot and gingham), EK Success (floral and text vellum) and K & Company (pink floral); *Date stamp:* Making Memories; *Stamping ink:* VersaColor, Tsukineko; *Embossing enamel:* Suze Weinberg; *Computer fonts:* Carpenter, downloaded from the Internet; CK Chemistry, "Fresh Fonts" CD, *Creating Keepsakes; Other:* Slide cover, rickrack and thread.

IDEA TO NOTE: To create the shiny letter "E" on her page, Hilary first cut the letter from cardstock. She then stamped the cardstock with red ink and heat embossed it with clear embossing powder.

AMBUSH: by Katherine Brooks
Supplies *Textured cardstock:* Bazzill Basics Paper; *Patterned papers:* Cross My Heart, 7gypsies and Anna Griffin; *Jigsaw letters, foam stamps and acrylic paint:* Making Memories; *Stamping ink:* ColorBox, Clearsnap; *Gel medium:* Delta Technical Coatings; *Rubber stamps:* Hero Arts; *Brads and eyelets:* Creative Impressions; *Computer font:* CK Scratchy, "Creative Clips & Fonts for Everyday Celebrations" CD, *Creating Keepsakes; Other:* Ribbon.

IDEA TO NOTE: Katherine created her background by machine stitching different sized strips of cardstock and patterned paper. Says Katherine, "When using your sewing machine, choose a needle that is suitable for stitching through leather or denim. A stronger need will not break when stitching several layers of cardstock or stitching through chipboard."

Hand stitching

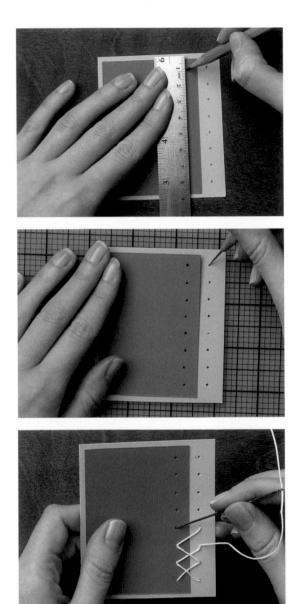

Step 1:

■ For completely even stitches, make faint pencil marks at even intervals. (Hint: Templates are also available to aid with this step.)

Step 2:

■ Using a large needle or paper piercer, punch holes into the cardstock, choosing a size to accommodate the thread (or other material, such as ribbon or yarn) you'll be using to sew.

Step 3:

■ Use a needle to make backstitches or "X"s across the cardstock. Or if using a stiff material, like jute, simply thread it through the holes by hand. Knot in back to secure.

VARIATIONS • • • *Dress up designs with other embroidery stitches such as chain stitches, daisies or French knots.*

Supplies *String:* Waxy Flax, Scrapworks.

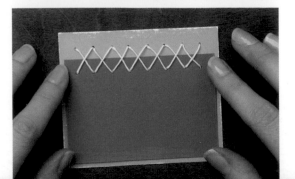

COZY

Since learning to read independently, I have to keep an eye on Nina. Instead of eating breakfast, she reads. Instead of doing chores, she reads. Instead of watching tv, she reads. Well, I'm ok with that one! I love the little reading nest she makes in her bed with all the blankets and pillows. Just so. So cozy!

Signs we were in love

- We went out to eat a lot & he always paid, but it wasn't "a date"
- We would talk for hours on the phone
- We always found "a reason" to need to drop by eachothers home

it must be Love

these pictures were taken just a month before our first kiss; back when we were "just friends". february 1999

COZY: by Elizabeth Ruuska
Supplies *Textured cardstock:* Bazzill Basics Paper; *Patterned paper:* KI Memories; *Vellum:* Autumn Leaves; *Lettering template:* Paige, QuicKutz; *Circle tag:* Avery; *Pen:* Pigment Pro, American Crafts; *Embroidery floss:* DMC; *Other:* Fabric.

IT MUST BE LOVE: by Megan Jones
Supplies *Patterned papers:* Carolee's Creations and Wordsworth; *Pens:* Zig Millennium, EK Success; Gelly Roll, Sakura; *Other:* Embroidery floss.

Using shrink plastic

Stop searching for the perfect charm or acrylic accent to suit your layout—just create your own! With a bit of shrink plastic and some inks, stamps or chalks, you can design adorable, durable embellishments directly suited for your page theme.

Step 1:

■ Stamp, draw or print an image onto a sheet of shrink plastic and add color, if desired. (Hint: The design will shrink to 20%–30% of the original size, so plan your image accordingly. Colors will also be intensified on the finish product.) If you'd like a hole in your accent, punch it now, again making note of how much it will shrink.

Step 2:

■ To shrink, follow the directions on the package. (Some brands require oven baking, while others will work with a heat gun.)

Step 3:

■ After the image shrinks and while it's still hot, place a glass (or any other heavy object with a smooth bottom) over the piece to flatten completely.

Supplies *Stamp and bead chain:* Making Memories.

Shovel the sand into the bucket, dump the bucket out and start the whole process over again. I think it would have taken you a while to notice if you were the only one on the beach. It was very difficult to coax you to leave.

Ocean **BEACH** Park

through the years LOVE

It's been over 50 years since the day Nana was cruising down Main Street with her girlfriend in Lubbock, Texas, on the lookout for good looking boys! Together, she and Granddad have been through wars, & births, deaths & dangerous accidents. It has been years since Nana has had to worry whether Granddad is lost in a Louisiana swamp with her sons, or has fallen off a mountainside on his dirt bike. Now they have new worries, whether Nana will walk again after breaking her hip, and what effects Granddad's stroke will have on him. But through it all, they have been, and will continue to be, together.
Photo taken in Feb. 2004

LEBENSFREUDE (JOY IN LIFE): by Amber Ries
Supplies *Textured cardstock:* Bazzill Basics Paper; *Patterned papers:* BasicGrey and Creative Imaginations; *Ribbon:* May Arts; *Stickers:* Jolee's Boutique, Sticko for EK Success; *Chalk:* EK Success; *Computer font:* Mordred, downloaded from the Internet; *Other:* Brads.

IDEA TO NOTE: The hearts on this layout were made with shrink plastic and painted to match the colors in the title.

OCEAN BEACH PARK: by Ashley Gull
Supplies *Patterned paper:* Making Memories; *Shrink plastic:* Grafix; *Corner punch:* Marvy Uchida; *Pen:* Sharpie; *Computer fonts:* AL Eyewitness and AL Modern Type, "Typewriter" CD, Autumn Leaves; Adler, downloaded from the Internet.

IDEA TO NOTE: The beautiful letters in Ashley's title are made from shrink plastic.

Using stamping ink

Stamping ink—it's not just for stamps anymore! Use dye, pigment and solvent varieties to dress up plain accents, design custom backgrounds, transform the color of pre-made embellishments and much more. While each technique produces heavy-duty results, the workload is surprisingly light. Discover the simplicity of these inking and tool techniques:

BRAYER

Step 1:
■ Create custom backgrounds by rolling a hard rubber brayer directly over inkpads or by coloring random stripes around the roller with markers.

Step 2:
■ Roll back and forth over cardstock until the desired effect is achieved.

VARIATIONS • • • *Produce different finishes by wrapping the roller with various objects, such as rubber bands or string, before inking. An inked brayer can also be used to change the color of ribbon, twill tape and more by running it over the surface.*

DIRECT TO PAPER

Step 1:
■ Cradle an ink pad in the palm of your hand.

Step 2:
■ Holding the cardstock, die cut or other accent in the other hand, lightly sweep the inkpad directly across the surface or along the edges to add a bit of shabby color.

Step 3:
■ Repeat with several shades of ink until the desired finish is achieved.

VARIATIONS • • • *Use inkpads to change the color of ribbon, twill tape and more. Simply hold the edge of the pad against the ribbon and pull the ribbon through. Repeat to build up color.*

Supplies *Die Cut:* Deluxe Designs; *Stamping ink:* Distress Ink, Ranger Industries.

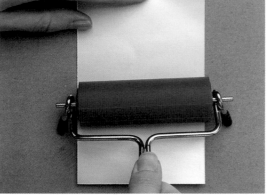

RESIST

Step 1:

■ Stamp image onto glossy cardstock with watermark ink. Use a heat gun to set the ink.

Step 2:

■ Coat a brayer with dye ink and roll over the surface repeatedly until the "ghosted" design comes through.

VARIATION • • • *You can also create this effect by heat embossing an image with white powder on white cardstock and color washing with watercolors or sponging ink over the top. (See p. 236.)*

Supplies *Stamp:* Hero Arts.

SPONGING AND STIPPLING

Step 1:

■ Create custom backgrounds by pressing a makeup, sea or kitchen sponge or stippling brush onto an inkpad. Lightly dab edges on scrap paper to remove excess ink.

Step 2:

■ Pounce sponge or brush onto cardstock until the desired shade and texture is achieved.

VARIATIONS • • • *For an abstract, marbled look, try sponging onto glossy paper and spritzing with water, allowing colors to blend and run.*

On the road between the houses of friends grass does not grow.

— Norwegian proverb

I was trying to put my finger on it, and then it hit me. This photo, taken at Jana's in the spring of 2004, speaks volumes about our friendship. The truth is, it doesn't really matter what's happening in either of our lives when we're together – though we may spend hours laughing and crying and everything in between over the drama of the day, in the end, there is an inexpressible comfort and safety and joy in just being together, and in having a special somebody to lean on. Yes, this photo says it all. And, yes, this is definitely my best friend.

FOREVER

BEST FRIENDS

BEST FRIEND: by Maya Opavska
Supplies *Textured paper:* Club Scrap; *Photo turn:* 7gypsies; *Chipboard letters:* Li'l Davis Designs; *Pen:* Fabrico, Tsukineko; *Brad:* Creative Imaginations; *Foam stamp, flowers, staples and ribbon:* Making Memories; *Rubber stamps:* Postmodern Design; *Stamping ink:* VersaMagic, VersaColor, Fabrico and StazOn, Tsukineko; *Computer fonts:* 2Peas Sailboat, downloaded from *www.two-peasinabucket.com*; McBooHmk, downloaded from the Internet; *Other:* Thread.

Isaac, I'm not sure why you like to take your right arm out of your shirts and pajamas but 10 SECONDS after you get dressed your arm comes out. Zippers, buttons, snaps...no matter the closure, no matter fabric You have become the one armed little boy. In these pajamas this day you managed to make a small whole for your toe as well. You are bursting from the seams. MARCH 2004

OCT 0 4 2004

10 SECOND ESCAPE: by Allison Kimball
Supplies *Letter and number stamps:* Ma Vinci's Reliquary (numbers and large letters) and Stampin' Up! (small letters); *Stamping ink:* ColorBox, Clearsnap (background); StazOn, Tsukineko; *Pen:* Zig Millennium, EK Success; *Other:* Date stamp.

Using texture paste

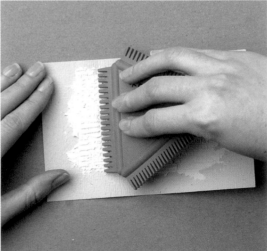

Did you ever think adding touchable texture would be simple? With mediums ranging from lightweight modeling to shimmering snow to tinted stucco pastes, changing the face of cardstock is as easy as spreading frosting on a cake. Just smear it, impress it, paint it and more...unlimited fashionable finishes await. Try the following:

CREATE PATTERNS

Step 1:

■ Stir paste until smooth. Using a palette knife, spread a thin layer onto thick cardstock or chipboard (some warping may occur). Replace the container lid to prevent the paste from drying out.

Step 2:

■ Drag a painter's comb, fork or a piece of chipboard cut with decorative scissors through the wet paste. Drag in a different direction for even more texture. Wash all tools immediately.

VARIATIONS • • • *Place a template, mesh or other open weave material over the cardstock and smear paste over the top of it. Allow to dry for a minute, then remove for a raised result.*

SWEET DREAMS: by Ashley Gull
Supplies *Patterned paper and rub-on:* Kopp Design; *Modeling paste:* Liquitex; *Corner punch:* Marvy Uchida; *Star stencil:* Stencibility.

IDEA TO NOTE: Ashley used texture paste to create the embossed stars on the background of her layout.

QUIET MOMENTS: by Margo Rogers
Supplies *Patterned paper:* BasicGrey; *Texture medium:* Texture Magic, Delta Technical Coatings; *Stencil:* Delta Technical Coatings; *Acrylic paint, rub-ons and tag:* Making Memories; *Photo turns:* 7gypsies; *Ribbon:* May Arts; *Stamping ink:* ColorBox, Clearsnap; *Brads:* Boxer Scrapbook Productions; *Metallic rub-ons:* Craf-T Products.

Painting over texture paste

Step 1:

■ Smooth paste onto cardstock and use a palette knife or other item to create a texture or pattern. Allow to dry completely.

Step 2:

■ Use acrylic paint, ink, chalk or rub-ons to add color to the surface.

VARIATIONS • • • *You can also add color by blending with a touch of acrylic paint before spreading onto cardstock or by using a palette knife to work paint into wet paste that has already been applied to cardstock.*

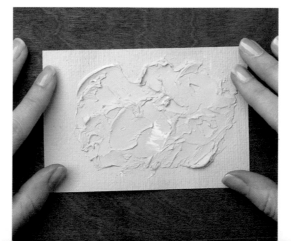

SPLASH: by Darcee Waddoups
Supplies *Texture template and shimmer paint:* Carolee's Creations; *Page pebbles:* Making Memories; *Acrylic squares:* Creek Bank Creations; *Dimensional adhesive:* Diamond Glaze, JudiKins.

Summer came on gentle winds
With the fragrance she ensares,
Trees now spread their leafy arms,
Bending with green she wears.
There is a hum of birds and bees,
Now the air is filled with song.
Bluest skies have foamy clouds
Drifting lazily along.
Linger summer, do not go.
You are hastening away.
All too soon these days will be
Memories of yesterday.

Linger Summer

LINGER SUMMER: by Shannon Taylor
Supplies *Patterned paper and silk flowers:* Rusty Pickle; *Metal mesh:* Making Memories; *Acrylic paint:* Ceramcoat, Delta Technical Coatings; *Dimensional adhesive:* Diamond Glaze, JudiKins; *Poem:* Agnes Davenport Bond, downloaded from *www.twopeasinabucket.com*; *Metal flower:* Making Memories; *Button:* Junkitz; *Adhesive:* Super Tape, Therm O Web; *Computer fonts:* President (journaling) and Jikharev (title), downloaded from the Internet; *Other:* Fabric.

Stamping into texture paste

Step 1:

■ Smooth an extra thin layer of paste onto cardstock. Allow to dry for a few minutes.

Step 2:

■ Press an inked or uninked stamp onto the surface. Remove and wash it immediately. (Hint: If the stamp is not leaving a clean impression, allow the clay to dry a bit longer. If the stamp will not press into the surface, reduce the drying time.)

Supplies *Metal stamps:* Making Memories.

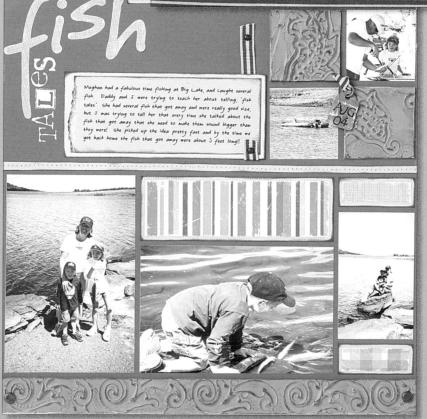

GOTTA LOVE 'EM: by Maya Opavska
Supplies *Patterned paper:* Daisy D's Paper Co.; *Textured paper:* Hanko Designs; *Photo turns and clips:* 7gypsies; *Rubber stamps:* Stampin' Up! ("love") and Stampers Anonymous (collage); *Ribbon:* May Arts; *Brads:* Scrap Arts; *Hole template:* Timeless Touches; *Stamping ink:* Brilliance, Tsukineko; *Pen:* Fabrico, Tsukineko; *Computer fonts:* CK Bella, "The Best of Creative Lettering" CD Combo, CK Cosmopolitan and CK Invitation, Becky Higgins' "Creative Clips & Fonts for Special Occasions" CD, CK Chemistry, "Fresh Fonts" CD, *Creating Keepsakes; Other:* Velvet and thread.

IDEA TO NOTE: Maya created her page accent by stamping images into the velvet. She used a rubber stamp and a hot iron.

FISH TALES: By Katherine Brooks
Supplies *Textured cardstock:* Bazzill Basics Paper; *Patterned paper:* Chatterbox; *Texture medium:* Texture Magic, Delta Technical Coatings; *Metal colorant:* Rub 'n Buff, Amaco; *Foam stamps:* Making Memories; *Stamping ink:* ColorBox, Clearsnap; *Acrylic paint:* Delta Technical Coatings; *Rubber stamps:* Hero Arts; *Brads:* Creative Impressions; *Walnut ink:* Fiber Scraps; *Jump ring:* Junkitz; *Rub-ons:* Autumn Leaves; *Computer font:* CBX-Watson, Journaling Font CD, Chatterbox; *Other:* Ribbon, mini tag and chipboard.

mini books & gift albums

For an interesting change of pace, try scrapbooking on a smaller scale—use all of your tools and techniques to design some creative mini albums. Not only are they relatively quick, a great place to experiment with new ideas and the ideal way to use up excess supplies and photos, but smaller albums are also perfect as interactive page elements or as gifts for loved ones. Take a look at the following examples that illustrate a variety of mini book subjects and styles.

TYPES OF ALBUMS

Mini albums are available in a variety of styles… choose one that will suit the size and subject matter of your project. Here are some suggestions:

Pre-made spiral-bound or stapled albums. *Often featuring chipboard or heavy cardstock covers, these are available in various shapes and sizes ranging from 2 x 2 inches all the way up to 9 x 9. Side-loading page protectors are also offered for most styles to slip on and protect the permanently-bound layouts.*

Three-ring binders. *Though half-pint albums are the most common smaller size, office supply stores also offer tiny three-ring notebooks that can accommodate several custom-cut pages.*

Cut cardstock. *Produce your own mini album easily by cutting a 12x12 sheet of cardstock in half, then folding each piece in half to form a square. Punch holes along the fold and bind several pieces together with ribbon, jute, staples or fasteners.*

Accordion-fold cardstock. *By trimming, folding (back and forth, like a fan) and combining pieces of cardstock, you can create custom pull-out albums as gifts or page accents. Design your own "cover" from chipboard, slide mounts, tags and more.*

Tags. *Fashion a quick mini book by adorning shipping tags with photos, embellishments and text, then binding them together with ribbon, bead chain, long bolts, fasteners or metal rings.*

ALBUM THEMES

Although mini books are ideal for showcasing a few favorite photos "just because," the smaller format also lends itself well to theme and gift albums. If you're stumped for subjects, try one of the following:

ABC Books

All About Me At Age…

Anniversary

Collections

Day Trips

Family Traditions

Favorites

Holidays

Hopes And Dreams

Inspirational Ideas

Meaningful Quotes And Poems

Mother, Father or Grandparents' Day

Parties

Pets

Recipes

School Achievements, Photos Or Projects

Scrapbook Rooms, Goals Or Achievements

Seasons

Sports

Tribute To Friends Or Loved Ones

CALIFORNIA DREAMING: by Lilia Meredith

Supplies *Textured cardstock:* Bazzill Basics Paper Co.; *Patterned paper:* Rusty Pickle and Chronicles, Deluxe Designs; *Punches:* EK Success; *Stickers:* Nostalgiques (postage) and Jolee's Boutique (shaker frame), EK Success; *Pen:* Sharpie; *Mini brads:* Lost Art Treasures; *Silver frame, leather frame, safety pin, tags, circle and heart clips:* Making Memories; *Ribbon:* May Arts and C. M. Offray & Son; *Vellum envelope:* Silver Crow Creations; *Mini frame charm and jump rings:* 7gypsies; *Label tape:* Dymo; *Negative strips:* Narratives, Creative Imaginations; *Acrylic paint:* Delta Technical Coatings; *Computer font:* CK Constitution, "Fresh Fonts" CD, *Creating Keepsakes; Other:* Key rings, rickrack trim, beverage coasters and a silk flower.

IDEA TO NOTE: Use beverage coasters from a dollar store as the front and back covers for your mini album. Spray them with a deacidification spray like Archival Mist if you're concerned with archival issues.

ALBUMS

MEMORIES TO GO: by Valerie Salmon
Supplies *Patterned paper, stickers, rub-on letters
and clasp:* Studio K, K & Company; *Metal-rimmed
tag:* Avery; *Jump ring:* Making Memories; *Ribbon:*
C. M. Offray & Son; *Takeout box die:* Accu-Cut;
Computer font: 2Peas Jack Frost, downloaded from
www.twopeasinabucket.com; *Other:* Crochet thread
and staples.

IDEAS TO NOTE: Make a gift grandparents will
love! Accordion-style, fold a 12 x 2 strip of patterned paper into six sections. For extra strength,
adhere a strip of 12 x 2 cardstock to the patterned
paper before folding. Cut a mini take-out box from
cardstock-weight patterned paper.

SWORDS FAMILY TIME CAPSULE: by Dana Swords
Supplies *Patterned paper:* Anna Griffin and
Chatterbox; *Die cuts:* Anna Griffin; *Rubber Stamps:*
All Night Media; *Stamping ink and mini brads:*
Stampin' Up!; *Mesh:* Avant Card; *Tag:* Rusty Pickle;
Computer fonts: Book Antiqua and Tahoma,
Microsoft Word; *Other:* Fabric and rickrack trim.

IDEA TO NOTE: Create a mini album time capsule.
Fashion accordion-style brochures about the important people and events in your everyday life.
Include photos of your family members, pets and
home, your children's stamped hand and foot-
prints, children's artwork, receipts for common
items, favorite recipes, special mementos and

notes from loved ones. Enclose the items inside a
clean, empty paint can covered with patterned
paper and embellishments. Apply a layer of Mod
Podge as a protective coating. Instead of burying
it, store it in a clean, dry place like the back of a
closet. Write the date to open the time capsule on
the outside of the can.

special memories - special moments

The Swords Family

Time Capsule

a bridge to the future

our hopes and dreams

links to the past... links to the past

the good stuff

Do not open until 2024

Notes
My Home
Cost of Ho
Addres
Squ
2004

Carlie

KENNA'S COLOR BOOK: by Melanie Joy Sovereen

Supplies *Patterned paper:* All My Memories; *Die cuts:* Cock-A-Doodle Design (bugs), O' Scrap (flowers); *Metal accents, buttons and mini brads:* All My Memories; *Computer fonts:* Monotype Corsiva, Microsoft Word and CK Corral, "Fresh Fonts" CD, *Creating Keepsakes; Ribbon:* C. M. Offray & Son; *Heart eyelets:* Baby Eyelets; *Mesh:* Maruyama, Magenta; *Die-cut letters:* QuicKutz; *Square conchos and printed pink die cuts:* Scrapworks

IDEA TO NOTE: Apply a thin layer of dimensional adhesive to your letter stickers or die cuts for a glossy, raised finish.

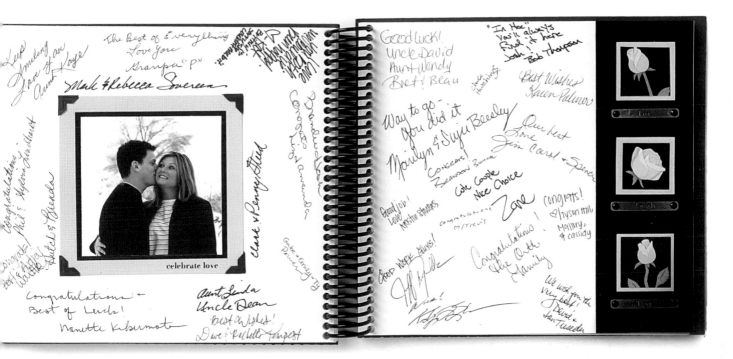

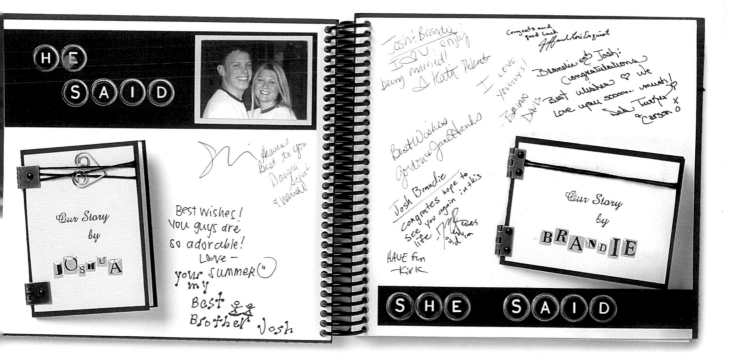

LINARES 2004: by Melanie Joy Sovereen
Supplies *Textured cardstock:* Bazzill Basics Paper Co.; *Bookplate:* K & Company; *Flower stickers, metal accents and mini brads:* All My Memories; *Letter stickers:* All My Memories (circle) and K & Company; *Hinges and heart clip:* Making Memories; *Embroidery floss:* DMC.

IDEA TO NOTE: Create a personalized guest book for an upcoming wedding. Leave plenty of room for guests to sign their names and write notes to the happy couple.

THE ENCYCLOPEDIA OF SCRAPBOOKING

cards

From eyelets to embossing, the techniques showcased in this book are not only useful, enjoyable and inspiring, but incredibly versatile. Let them take you beyond scrapbooking—apply your new-found (or enhanced) knowledge to create some imaginative greeting cards and paper crafts, as well. Consider the way the following card samples make use of a variety of scrapbooking tools and techniques and discover how you can mix and match to produce your most-impressive creations yet.

FATHER'S DAY: by Denise Pauley
Supplies *Alphabet stamps:* Hero Arts; *Compass stamp:* PSX Design; *Stamping ink:* Versamark, Brilliance and StazOn, Tsukineko; *Embossing powder:* Ranger Industries; *Leafing pen:* Krylon; *Aluminum plant tags:* Anima Designs; *Epoxy stickers:* Art Warehouse, Creative Imaginations; *Eyelets and bead chain:* Making Memories.

BIRTHDAY: by Denise Pauley
Supplies *Patterned paper:* American Crafts; *Sticker, hinge, ribbon and tag:* Making Memories; *Rubber stamp:* Impress Rubber Stamps; *Stamping ink:* StazOn, Tsukineko; *Acrylic paint:* Plaid Enterprises; *Other:* Packing tape.

for my father

FOR MY FATHER: by Gail Robinson
Supplies *Corrugated paper:* DMD, Inc.; *Book-themed fabric:* Makings; *Fusible web:* Wonder Under, Pellon; *Bookplate and eyelet letter:* Making Memories; *Gold fiber:* DMC; *Beads:* Wal-Mart; *Tinted walnut ink:* Tsukineko; *Acrylic paint:* Delta Technical Coatings; *Quote: Quote, Unquote,* Autumn Leaves; *Computer font:* CK Heritage, "Creative Clips & Fonts for Special Occasions"; *Other:* Brads.

IDEAS TO NOTE: Get the soft look of suede by spraying Tsukineko's Eucalyptus-tinted walnut ink on white cardstock. Consider using fabric on your project for a luxurious feel.

PARTY: by Joannie McBride
Supplies *Patterned paper:* Kopp Design; *Ribbon and pocket:* Li'l Davis Design; *Paper and leather flowers:* Making Memories; *Brads:* Karen Foster Design (round), Making Memories (square); *Pen:* Slick Writer, American Crafts.

TRUE LOVE FOREVER: by Gail Robinson
Supplies *Folder:* Autumn Leaves; *Tag punch:* Emagination Crafts; *Acrylic paint:* Delta Technical Coatings; *Letter stamps:* Close To My Heart; *Rub-on words:* Making Memories; *Label tape:* Dymo; *Button:* Doodlebug Design; *Ribbon:* C.M. Offray & Son; *Embroidery floss:* DMC; *Packing tape:* Scotch, 3M.

IDEAS TO NOTE: Create a custom sticker or page accent using any printed or photocopied image and the packing tape transfer technique. See page 217 for complete instructions. Attach ribbon to your project using the French knot embroidery stitch.

HAPPY BIRTHDAY: by Denise Pauley
Supplies *Patterned paper:* Creative Imaginations; *Alphabet stamps:* PSX Design; *Stamping ink:* StazOn, Tsukineko and Fresco, Stampa Rosa; *Chalk:* Deluxe Designs; *Punch flowers and gems:* Beaded Wire Whims, Creative Imaginations; *Eyelets:* Making Memories.

HAVE A VERY MERRY: by Gail Robinson
Supplies *Textured cardstock:* Bazzill Basics Paper Co.; *Patterned paper:* KI Memories; *Frame, metal sheet and acrylic paint:* Making Memories; *Transparency:* HammerMill; *Ribbon:* C. M. Offray & Son; *Buckle:* Li'l Davis Designs; *Computer font:* Arial Black, Microsoft Word.

IDEA TO NOTE: Place a printed transparency over a metal sheet. When trimming the transparency, be sure to leave it large enough to cover entire metal sheet to ensure a clean, sleek look.

THINKING OF YOU: by Joannie McBride
Supplies *Patterned paper and memory file accent:* Daisy D's Paper; *Fabric strip:* Nostalgiques, EK Success; *Canvas paper:* me and my BIG ideas; *Paper flower and square brad:* Making Memories; *Stamping ink:* Tsukineko; *Pen:* Slick Writer, American Crafts.

POINSETTIA: by Denise Pauley
Supplies *Specialty paper:* Black Ink; *Cork:* Magic Scraps; *Stamping ink:* Nick Bantock, Ranger Industries; *Metallic rub-ons:* Craf-T Products; *Walnut ink:* Postmodern Design; *Ribbon:* Bobbin Ribbon; *Brads:* Making Memories; *Other:* Eyelet.

BOO TO YOU: by Denise Pauley
Supplies *Mesh:* Maruyama, Magenta; *Alphabet stamps:* PSX Design; *Stamping ink:* StazOn, Tsukineko; *Tag:* Foofala; *Rub-ons:* Creative Imaginations; *Zipper, jump ring and zipper pull:* Junkitz; *Charm:* Impress Rubber Stamps; *Eyelet:* Doodlebug Design.

OH BOY, OH BOY: by Gail Robinson
Supplies *Fabric tag, bookplate, safety pins, metal corners and plaque:* Making Memories; *Twill tape:* Scenic Route Paper Co.; *Rubber stamp:* Close To My Heart; *Acrylic paint:* Delta Technical Coatings; *CD and CD holder:* Sony; *Computer fonts:* CK Argyle, "Heritage, Retro & Vintage Collection" CD and CK Cute, "Creative Clips & Fonts by Becky Higgins" CD, *Creating Keepsakes.*

IDEAS TO NOTE: Use your scrapbooking skills to create a custom lullaby CD complete with a homemade card that fits in the CD booklet slot. Adhere the bookplate to the front of the CD case for a fun dimensional look.

LET IT SNOW: by Denise Pauley
Supplies *Specialty Paper:* Creative Imaginations; *Alphabet stamps:* PSX Design; *Stamping ink:* StazOn, Tsukineko and Fresco, Stampa Rosa; *Acrylic paint:* Delta Technical Coatings; *Metal tiles, ribbon and jump rings:* Making Memories; *Tags:* Avery Dennison.

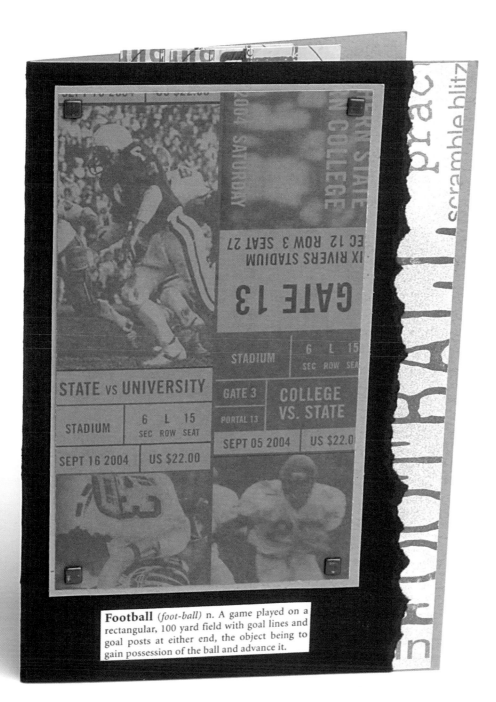

FOOTBALL: by Joannie McBride
Supplies *Patterned papers:* Karen Foster Design (ticket collage), Carolee's Creations (football words); *Football definition:* Karen Foster Design; *Quote and ticket stubs:* Daisy D's Paper; *Square brads:* Making Memories.

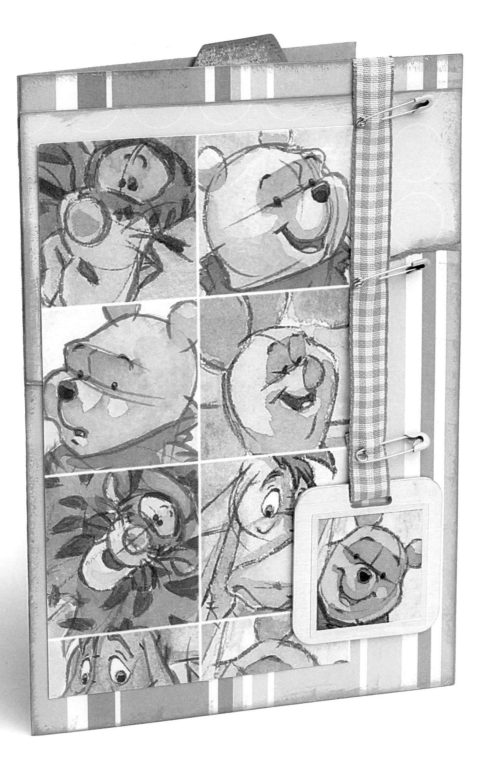

WINNIE THE POOH: by Joannie McBride
Supplies *Patterned papers:* Kopp Design (striped and blue), Sandylion (Winnie the Pooh); *Metal tag and stickers:* Kopp Design; *Ribbon:* Li'l Davis Designs; *Diaper pins:* Making Memories; *Stamping ink:* Tsukineko; *Pen:* Slick Writer, American Crafts; *tab:* Creekbank Creations.

BE MINE: by Denise Pauley
Supplies *Stamping ink:* StazOn, Tsukineko; *Die cuts:* Sizzix, Provo Craft; *Ephemera:* Foofala; *Ribbon, brads and eyelet:* Making Memories; *Key:* Lil' Davis Designs; *Alphabet buttons:* Junkitz; *Other:* Playing card.

FALL: by Denise Pauley
Supplies *Specialty paper:* Black Ink; *Patterned paper:* Creative Imaginations; *Rub-ons and ribbon:* Making Memories; *Stamping ink:* Nick Bantock, Ranger Industries; *Charm:* Embellish It! Boutique Trims.

appendix

archival basics

The term archival may conjure up images of a gray-haired, white-gloved preservationist working in a musty collections section of a library, but, luckily for scrapbookers, archival products have spread into the scrapbooking industry, allowing memories to be preserved to last the test of time.

Not all of the techniques illustrated in this book are archivally safe. The choice of whether to strictly follow the guidelines here or not, is a personal decision. If you want to ensure your photos and memorabilia will be safe for future generations, follow the guidelines below:

Photos

A great photograph is the key ingredient to whipping up a great page design. Below are some tips for keeping your photographs in great shape for a long time.

If you choose to label the back of your photos, use a soft graphite pencil, a fine-line marker or a permanent pen. Never use a ballpoint pen as it can cause impressions in the picture. All ink used for scrapbooking purposes should be waterproof, odorless when dry, permanent, quick drying, non-bleeding, non-toxic and fade resistant. Ideally, it is best to avoid writing on the back of one-of-a-kind photos.

Store photos in acid- and lignin-free boxes in a dark, cool and dry environment. Acid used to be commonly added during the paper-making process to more easily break the wood fiber into pulp, but paper mills are beginning to shy away from it as the EPA establishes standards and more people begin demanding acid-free paper. If paper is made with acid, it will seep into any photos or documents you scrapbook and damage them. Lignin is a naturally occurring binding substance found in plant material that can chemically degrade paper, causing discoloration.

When handling photos, wash your hands frequently to avoid transferring your natural skin oils to the photographs. In the case of one-of-a-kind photos, consider wearing cotton gloves

The images on black-and-white photos last longer than those in color photos because the dyes in color photographs break down over time, causing the colors to fade. When developing black-and-white photos, keep in mind there are two paper types: Resin-coated paper has a polyethylene (plastic) backing and is the most common, but doesn't last as long as fiber-based paper which has a paper backing and has the longest life span of any print.

Products

With the variety of great scrapbooking products on the market, how can you find products that are safe for archival scrapbooking? Acid-free does not always mean the product is photo-safe. The most common and reliable test to predict harmful chemical reactions between scrapbooking materials and photographic images is the Photographic Activity Test (PAT). Developed by Image Permanence Institute, this test is performed by various manufacturers and predicts possible interactions between photographic images and the enclosures in which they are stored. If a product passes the PAT, it simply means that the material is safe for use with photographs, but not necessarily archival. It is a good idea to make sure the product has also been pH tested.* Below are some tips for selecting commonly used scrapbooking products.

Any paper product you use should be acid- and lignin free and buffered (a process that adds a buffering agent to the paper, controlling the pH level from changing over time.)

Adhesives should be removeable, colorless, odorless and solid. Never use rubber cement or magnetic photo albums. Products to consider include photo corners, glue sticks, glue dots and double-sided tape.

Different kinds of metal will react in various ways with paper and photographs. It is best to use a coated metal and to be cautious of sharp edges that could scratch or mar photos.

Use only lead-free paint. Be cautious with water-soluble paint as it can fade and also run or bleed through to other pages.

Be aware when using natural products such as cork, bark, leaves or flowers, that all of these materials contain lignin and will discolor your pages over time.

Select rubber stamp ink that is pigment-based as opposed to dye-based. Not only are dye colors generally less stable over the long-term, they are soluble while pigment colors are non-soluble. Always powder emboss the ink to prevent the color from fading or changing over time.

Stickers should be judged by the same criteria used for selecting paper and adhesives. The sticker should be acid- and lignin-free and buffered and the adhesive should meet the safety guidelines of a good adhesive.

Preserving Original Documents

Many times, scrapbookers come across unique treasures from the past or current items such as a newspaper article, certificate or letter that they may want to use in a layout design. Here are several options for safely scrapbooking such items.

Newspaper articles can be washed to deacidify the paper by letting the article soak in distilled water in a shallow dish for 20 minutes. Let the paper dry and store in an acid-free environment.

For certificates, letters or larger newsprint items, you can use deacidification spray. Certificates and other documents cannot be washed because they often have ink on them that will run or bleed.

Never use glue or tape on valuable paper documents or fiber-based black-and-white photos. Use safe mounting corners.

Another alternative, is to scan the item and print it out. It is ideal to use a laser printer, but an inkjet printer can be used. It is best to use the manufacturer recommended printer/ink/paper combinations and pigment ink is a better choice than dyes. Find out if the manufacturer of your printer has conducted longevity testing of their printer inks to see which combinations are best for you.

If you are still concerned about using original photos, scanning photos and original documents provides a digital method of scrapbooking and your photos and documents can be tucked away in an archival-safe photo box or organization system.

These are some of the basics of safely preserving your memories. There are many other resources available for more information – see the list below. Happy scrapbooking and remember to keep it safe!

"SOS Saving Our Scrapbooks" by Creating Keepsakes

Scrapbook Preservation Society – www.scrapbookpreservationsociety.com

American Institute for Conservation of Historic and Artistic Works – www.aic.faic.org

Library of Congress Preservation Directorate – www.loc.gov/preserv

Wilhelm Imaging Research – www.wilhelmresearch.com

* It may also be helpful to look for products that have the CK OK Seal of Approval, as these products have met specific requirements to ensure a safe product.

photo organization

It's every scrapbooker's worst nightmare (or greatest opportunity)—a pile of unorganized snapshots spanning several events, seasons or years. If you're overwhelmed by the backlog, get the stacks sorted to give yourself easy access when you're inspired to create! Get focused on photos with three simple steps:

Sift and Sort

To avoid repeated searches for a few usable shots, begin by dividing the surplus into three piles:

TOSSERS: Get rid of out-of-focus, badly-lit or generally unusable shots permanently so you won't waste any more time needlessly shuffling through them.

EXTRAS: Pull the marginal photos that you simply don't deem "scrapworthy." Store this batch separately or give the pictures to family members, use them in gift albums or let your kids experiment with them during craft time.

KEEPERS: Select the photos that best represent each event or moment. These don't always have to be stellar, award-winning shots, but they should be pictures that successfully evoke memories, capture moods, record pieces of family history...or simply inspire you to scrapbook!

Classify the Keepers

Once you've pulled the shots most likely to appear on layouts, break them into smaller groups so the sought-after photos will be immediately accessible when you're working on a particular album, event or subject. Try filing them by:

DATE: Sort into piles by month or year if you scrapbook chronologically (or simply have a lot of photos you're not likely to work on soon). Use an archivally-safe photo marking pen to note pertinent information on the back of key photos.

EVENT OR THEME: File photos by holidays, seasons, vacations or other events. When you're motivated to design birthday pages or find a stash of themed embellishments you're eager to use, for example, just pull the corresponding photos and complete layouts for several years at once.

FAMILY MEMBER: Create individual groups for each member of your family that include event or everyday photos that feature them prominently. If you get a layout or journaling idea pertaining to your significant other, for example, you can quickly find photos to suit it.

LAYOUT: If you're great at visualizing well ahead of time, separate photos based on future layouts. Though this is more time consuming, the result will be smaller batches of photos that can be pulled and scrapbooked at a moment's notice.

PROJECT: If you work on individual albums for family, children, grandparents, holidays or vacations, group photos according to the album in which they'll appear. Each stack can also be sub-sorted into specific subjects.

Select Storage

Now that your photos are categorized into manageable groups, the proper storage system can help you remember what you've got and where to find it. Here are a few tried-and-true methods:

ALBUMS: If it may be awhile before you scrap your photos, keep them stored in non-magnetic albums. Pictures can be slipped into pockets until needed and the format allows your family to enjoy the photos even before they're on layouts.

PAGE PROTECTORS OR ENVELOPES: Place pictures grouped for individual layouts in page protectors along with design notes and any corresponding memorabilia or journaling ideas. If you need to shop for paper or embellishments, simply take the pack to the store to match materials. Store these in a three-ring binder until you're ready to scrap.

PHOTO CASES: Large photo storage cases, totes or boxes allow you to collect hundreds of photos. Use smaller plastic containers, divider tabs or envelopes to keep categories separated.

POST-ITS: Use Post-Its to group photos for individual layouts. Stick adhesive to the back of one photo and wrap it around the rest. Use the paper to include notes about the event, potential design, title and journaling ideas. Store these batches in photo boxes, baskets or divided organizers.

To give your newly-created system a shot at success, be sure to maintain it—each time you print a batch of photos or get a roll back from the developer, sort and file immediately. Diligent photo organization is your secret weapon to more productive scrap sessions!

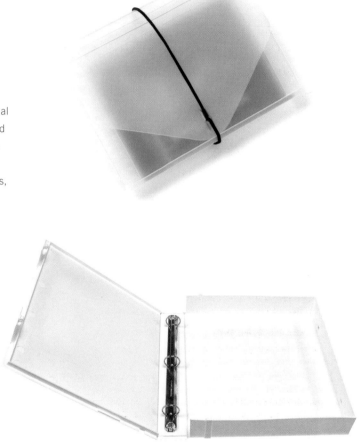

space organization

Once you've established a space to scrapbook, devise the perfect set up to suit your design process. A little organization can go a long way towards increasing your creativity and productivity. When arranging your studio:

- Go vertical if space is limited. Use stackable storage units to maximize your capacity.
- Place often-used supplies within arm's reach.
- Label drawers and containers to quickly find what you need.
- Use available wall space to display work. Hang corkboards to hold supplies, sketches and inspirational ideas.

Designating a place for everything (and keeping everything in its place) is the easiest way to keep supplies accessible. In addition to units designed specifically for scrapbooking, consider these options:

- **Cardstock/patterned paper.** Store horizontally in wire cubes, plastic trays or shop-style shelving units. House vertically in paper totes, drawer units, desktop document holders or in hanging folders in metal crates or carts.
- **Tools.** Try a revolving caddy, baskets (filled with dried beans to keep tools upright), tool boxes or pegboards where tools can be hung.
- **Pens/pencils.** Store markers horizontally in pen totes, plastic trays or baskets. Store pencils in boxes, buckets, revolving containers or pencil cases.
- **Flat supplies.** Keep stickers, templates, pre-mades and more in small paper totes, file folders or in page protectors within binders.
- **Small accents.** Store fasteners, beads, charms and more in bead, floss, tackle or button boxes, jars, watchmaker tins, stackable containers or baggies.
- **Medium/large accents.** Place plastic desk dividers in shallow drawers or use tilt tins, baskets or tackle boxes with customizable compartments.

- **Ribbon/fibers.** Try ribbon boxes, dowels, drawer units or plastic bins for spools; shorter strands pinned on a corkboard or in baggies attached with metal rings.
- **Stamps.** Store wood-mounted stamps in shallow drawer units, clear boxes, upright on shelves or in stackable box frames (punches can be similarly stored). Keep unmounted stamps in CD jewel cases, floss or tea bag boxes or tacked to cardboard within page protectors.
- **Ink pads.** Try cassette storage boxes or shallow drawer units.
- **Paints and art media.** Group them with applicators in plastic tubs, shoe or tackle boxes.
- **Photos.** Use inexpensive photo boxes, clear envelopes or shoeboxes divided by date, family member or event.
- **Magazines.** File by date on bookshelves, in magazine holders or baskets. Store favorite articles and layouts from older issues in a personal idea binder.

File supplies with a system that supports the way you select materials when designing a page. Are you driven by subject? Techniques? Tone? Analyze your answer and try one of these storage sorting solutions:

- **By product type.** Store similar supplies together to easily find the products you need.
- **By color.** Group everything by color family and go to one section to find all of the supplies you own in a specific color.
- **By theme.** Cluster supplies according to the colors, accents and patterns often associated with specific holidays, subjects or seasons.

■ **By manufacturer.** Keep each company's products together if you're most familiar with their product lines.

Now that your scrap studio is complete, keep it clutter-free! Vow to:

■ **Eliminate overflow.** When your storage containers are full, use some of your existing stash before buying new products.

■ **Prevent piles.** When you acquire new products, file them immediately. And, don't let unwanted supplies waste space—give them to charitable organizations or other scrapbookers.

■ **Clean up.** After major scrap sessions, put away unused items, file scraps and toss trash.

■ **Sift regularly.** Sort through containers every few months to eliminate products you haven't considered using.

journaling

If you enjoy designing layouts but agonize over the journaling, the following guide answers the whys, whats, hows, wheres and whens of the process. It may help you complete the story that your photos have just begun.

Why

Though you fondly remember the events and emotions captured in each photograph, future generations—and even your immediate family—may need a bit more detail to make sense of the memories. Including the facts and feelings behind each moment can turn your layout into a touching and valuable part of family history.

What

Journaling can be anything from a name and date to a lengthy love letter. Let your text reflect the tone you're creating for the page and the feelings that your photos evoke. If you're at a loss for words, ask yourself a few questions:

■ What event, tradition or season am I showcasing? What were the most heartwarming, hilarious or hectic moments? Were there any special, unphotographed incidents that I want to record?

■ If this photo was taken "just because," what led me to pick up my camera? What was I feeling as I took the picture?

■ What was my subject thinking? (Put yourself in their shoes and imagine how elated, sad, curious, contemplative or proud they are.)

■ Is there something historically or sentimentally special about this location?

■ Why is this photo so meaningful to me?

How

Although you can accompany photos with extensive, emotional journaling, there are additional ways to include heartfelt details. Try one of following journaling techniques:

■ **Lists.** Quickly summarize events, favorites, facts and more.

■ **Quotes.** Find the perfect quote, song lyric or poem to sum up your feelings.

■ **The words of others.** Hand the pen to your child, significant other, relative or friend and allow that person to supply the text.

■ **Captions.** Sometimes names, dates and locations are all you need to commemorate a particular event.

■ **Notes.** Jot a series of travel, love or reminder notes that include your thoughts, anecdotes or advice.

Where

While printing text directly onto the background or within a journaling box is the standard method, experiment with one of the following looks:

■ Add text to decorated tags, envelopes, die cuts and more.

■ Conceal additional personal journaling under hinged accents or within pockets, envelopes or on the back of your layout.

■ Surround your focal photo or layout with a border of text. Or, run journaling along one side or across the bottom of the page.

■ Print words on a transparency, vellum or tissue and place it over photos, memorabilia, patterned paper, textured designs and more.

■ Combine handwriting, fonts, stamps and stickers to design text that's fun as well as functional.

When

If you have trouble remembering details when it's time to journal, use one of these techniques to keep the memories fresh:

- Carry a small notebook in your purse or camera bag to record thoughts as events occur.
- If you keep a written journal, consult entries for your perspective on past events.
- Turn to your organizer, date book or PDA for dates and details that elude you.
- Look through old letters or e-mails that may have touched upon milestones or memories that you'd like to include.
- Keep a calendar on the refrigerator to note each day's important incidents, big and small.

P. 77

Although she complained that Rome smelled of roses and body odour, that it was hot and her feet hurt, I think Rome did Kylene good. The sunshine made her skin glow, the walking was good exercise and where else in the non-Italian world will you get delicious Gelato?
She played it cool, like it was no big deal; it was just another tiring trip with her brother-in-law who pushed her to her limits, and although they say "all roads lead to Rome", how many American women really do get the chance to travel to the city of the Holy See?

P. 221

My FAMILY is always there for me and supports me in everything I do!

I love my HAIR because it always seem to do what I want it to do. It's just wonderful!

My FRIENDS & I have our own jokes words. We have so much fun just hanging out!

P. 127

tale

the first time Jeremy saw these pictures he said, "you 'look like you're 'in a fairy tale." I replied, "I feel like I'm in one!" I'm just so happy with the life God has blessed me with. He sent me the man of my dreams followed by my little angel. I love

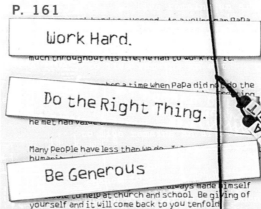

P. 161

Work Hard.

much throughout his life, he had to work for it.

...er a time when Papa did not do the

he met had value...

Do the Right Thing.

Many people have less than we do. I...
humani...

Be Generous

...always made himself
...ble to help at church and school. Be giving of yourself and it will come back to you tenfold

technology & computer

With the advent of personal computers, digital cameras, scanners and quality home printers, technology and scrapbooking have become partners in the quest for preserving precious family memories. You can snap a photo, download it to your computer, adjust the size and color, add type using photo-editing software, and print—all without leaving your house!

Impact & Benefits of Technology

If you're a strictly traditional scrapbooker you may wonder what benefits come from using your computer as a scrapbooking tool. Maybe you feel the information is too complicated. Or, perhaps you aren't ready to invest in new equipment. In reality, relying on your computer may actually simplify some steps as you create your pages. And, you might be surprised that it's not as expensive as you imagine.

Photo-Editing Software

In many ways, computers and digital photography offer you more control over your photos. Photo-editing software provides you the opportunity to crop, remove unwanted elements and restore damaged heritage photos. For scrapbookers concerned with preserving old family photos, fixing scratches, tears and discolorations are very valuable photo-editing tools. And, with recent advances in photo and printer technology, photo restoration can be done with the touch of a button. Now that is simple!

Digital Photography

Digital cameras are revolutionizing the way people take, store and reproduce their photos. Gone are the limits of 24- or 36-exposure rolls of film. With a digital camera you can take hundreds of photos before you'll have to download your memory card onto a computer. Once you've downloaded your images, most photo-editing programs give you the option to print your photos in custom or traditional sizes (4" x 6", 5" x 7" and wallets). In addition to at-home printing, online digital photo studios will develop your photos for you (including the option for poster size prints).

Computer-Generated Layouts

Scrapbookers have the option of creating completely digital layouts. Comprised of all digital elements, computer-generated layouts incorporate digital accents and faux textures. And, you have the option of archiving your layout digitally on a CD, in album creation software or printing it out to store in an album. These layouts and albums are easy to share with family and friends via e-mail and the Internet.

Online Community

The Internet has left its mark on the scrapbooking world. Scrapbooking websites offer information, inspiration and the opportunity to interact with a community of people who share your passion for creating layouts and preserving family history.

Let's take a brief look at some of the cool things you can do with your computer:

JOURNALING

- Choose from millions of fonts
- Select font colors and adjust type sizes
- Edit and spell check your document
- Print journaling directly onto cardstock, patterned paper, transparencies, etc.

PHOTO EDITING

- Enlarge, reduce, crop, and manipulate photos
- Restore damaged photos
- Add type and journaling onto photos
- Upload photos to photography websites

STORAGE

■ Organize and store your photos (and burn them to a CD for backup)

■ Store completed layouts

PAGE CREATION

■ Make unique type-based accents

■ Combine computer elements with traditional embellishments

■ Create entire pages on your computer using programs such as Adobe Photoshop Elements, Microsoft Picture It! or Paint Shop Pro

SHARING

■ Easily share photos and layouts with family and friends

■ Post layouts online to share with other scrapbookers

■ Chat with other scrapbookers around the world

Computers are here to stay! Embracing the partnership between computers and traditional paper scrapbooking will open the door to even more creativity.

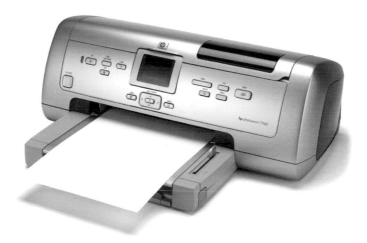

resource guide

Ready to shop for scrapbook products?
Consider the following options:

Local Stores

Look for scrapbook products at your local scrapbook, art supply, craft and hobby stores. Look in the Yellow Pages under the following headings: art supplies, craft, hobbies and collectibles, memory, paper, paper crafting, scrapbook, shopping and specialty retail. Try Qwest's Dex Online directory at *www.dexonline.com*.

Chain Stores

Many major discount and craft stores carry scrapbook products. Look for the following stores in your neighborhood:

A.C. Moore *www.acmoore.com*
Archivers *www.archiversonline.com*
Hobby Lobby *www.hobbylobby.com*
Jo-Ann Fabric & Crafts *www.joann.com*
Lewiscraft (Canada) *www.lewiscraft.ca*
Linens 'n Things *www.lnt.com*
Memories *www.memories.com*
Michaels *www.michaels.com*
Rag Shop *www.ragshop.com*
Recollections *www.recollectionsonline.com*
Target *www.target.com*
Walmart *www.walmart.com*
Xpedx *www.xpedx.com*

Online Stores

If your local scrapbook and craft stores don't carry the products you need, consider ordering them from an online store. Check out the following options:

A Peek Into Yesterday *www.apeekintoyesterday.com*
AccuCut *www.accucut.com*
Addicted to Rubber Stamps
www.addictedtorubberstamps.com
All Canadian Scrapbooks *www.allcdnscrapbooks.com*
All My Memories *www.allmymemories.com*

Auntie Dear Scrapbook Store *www.auntiedear.com*
Blockheads Paper Arts *www.blockheadstamps.com*
Brassworks Embossing *www.brassworksembossing.com*
California Stampin' & Scrapbooks *www.castampin.com*
Carolee's Creations & Company, LLC *www.ccpaper.com*
Chatterbox *www.chatterboxinc.com*
Clearsnap, Inc. *www.clearsnap.com*
Club Scrap *www.clubscrap.com*
Creative Circle Crafts *www.creativecirclecrafts.com*
Creative Cropping *www.creativecropping.com*
Crop In Style *www.cropinstyle.com*
Cropper Hopper *www.cropperhopper.com*
Croppin' Paradise *www.croppinparadise.com*
Daisy D's Paper Co. *www.daisydspaper.com*
Deluxe Designs *www.deluxedesigns.com*
Design Originals *www.d-originals.com*
Dick Blick Art Materials *www.dickblick.com*
Discount Scrap Supplies *www.discountscrapsupplies.com*
Discount Scrapbook Network
www.discountscrapbooknetwork.com
Dymo *www.dymo.com*
Ellison Craft & Design *www.ellison.com*
Emagination Crafts *www.emaginationcrafts.com*
Epson *www.epson.com*
Fiber Scraps *www.fiberscraps.com*
Fiskars *www.fiskars.com*
Fusion Art Stamps *www.fusionartstamps.com*
Get Crafts *www.getcrafts.com*
Glue Dots, Inc. *www.gluedots.com*
Gone Scrappin' *www.gonescrappin.com*
Harvest the Crop *www.harvestthecrop.com*
Hero Arts *www.heroarts.com*
Home Shopping Network *www.hsn.com*
Hot Off the Press *www.paperpizazz.com*
HP *www.hp.com*
Impress Rubber Stamps *www.impressrubberstamps.com*
In Joy Rubber Stamps *www.injoystamps.com*
Kolo Photo Albums *www.kolo.com*
Lexmark *www.lexmark.com*
Luv2Scrapbook *www.luv2scrapbook.com*

Ma Vinci's Reliquary *www.crafts.dm.net/mall/reliquary/*

Magic Scraps *www.magicscraps.com*

Marvy Uchida *www.uchida.com*

Maude Asbury *www.maudeasbury.com*

My Mind's Eye *www.frame-ups.com*

My Scrapbook Studio *www.myscrapbookstudio.com*

My Scrapbooking *www.myscrapbooking.com*

My Treasure Quest *www.mytreasurequest.com*

Ofoto *www.ofoto.com*

P.S. I Love You *www.brass-stencils.com*

Pam's Creations and Scrapbook Basics

www.pamscreations.net

Paper Addict *www.paperaddict.com*

Paper Cuts *www.papercuts.com*

Paper Style *www.paperstyle.com*

Polly's Pals *www.pollyspals.com*

Pressed Petals, Inc. *www.pressedpetals.com*

QVC *www.qvc.com*

R & R Scrapbooking *www.scrapbooking.ca*

Rubber Dream *www.rubberdream.com*

Scrapbook Essentials *www.scrapbookessentials.biz*

Scrap Addict, Inc. *www.scrapaddict.com*

Scrap This! *www.scrapthis.net*

Scrap Your Trip *www.scrapyourtrip.com*

Scrap Yourself Silly

www.scrapyourselfsilly.safeshopper.com

Scrapbook Express *www.scrapbookexpress.com*

Scrapbook Extravaganza *www.scrapbooksupplystore.com*

Scrapbook Hut *www.scrapbookhut.com*

Scrapbook Playground *www.scrapbookplayground.com*

ScrapbooKorner *www.scrapbookorner.com*

Scrapbooks by the Lake *www.scrapbooksbythelake.com*

ScrapCandy.com *www.scrapcandy.com*

ScraPlanet *www.scraplanet.com*

Scrap'n Stuff *www.scrapnstuff.com*

Scrappin' Angels *www.scrappinangels.com*

Scrappin' Friends *www.scrappinfriends.com*

Scrappin' Grannies *www.scrappingrannies.com*

Scrapping with Style *www.scrappingwithstyle.com*

Scraps Ahoy *www.scrapsahoy.com*

SEI *www.shopsei.com*

Shrinky Dinks *www.shrinkydinks.com*

Simply Stickers *www.simplystickers.com*

Simply Superb Scrapbooks

www.simplysuperbscrapbooks.com

Sizzix *www.sizzix.com*

Smead *www.retrospectbysmead.com*

Snapfish *www.snapfish.com*

Stamp In Ink *www.stampinink.com*

Stampstruck, Inc. *www.stampstruck.com*

Stickers Galore *www.stickersgalore.com*

Sunday International *www.sundayint.com*

Sweetwater *www.sweetwaterscrapbook.com*

The Little Scrapbook Store

www.thelittlescrapbookstore.com

The Stamp Attic *www.stampattic.com*

The Vintage Workshop *www.thevintageworkshop.com*

The Weathered Door *www.theweathereddoor.com*

Therm O Web *www.thermoweb.com*

Times to Cherish by Current *www.timestocherish.com*

Touch of Embossing *www.touchofembossing.com*

USArt Quest *www.usartquest.com*

Walnut Hollow *www.walnuthollow.com*

Xyron *www.xyron.com*

Direct Sales Companies

If you like attending or hosting home parties from direct
sales companies, consider the following companies:

Close to My Heart *www.closetomyheart.com*

Creative Memories *www.creativememories.com*

Stampin' Up! *www.stampinup.com*

glossary of terms

Whether you're a beginning, intermediate or advanced scrapbooker, you may stumble upon an expression or idea that's new to you. If you're searching for the definition of a basic scrapbooking tool, topic or technique, consult the following list:

a

Accent
Pre-made or handmade item used to embellish a scrapbook layout. Anything from a sticker or a pressed flower to a decorated tag or piece of metal mesh qualifies as an accent.

Acid-free
Products designated as "acid free" have a pH factor of 7 or greater (or 6.5 by industry standards). Acid-free materials, such as cardstock, are recommended for scrapbooking because contact with acidity can cause or hasten a photo's decay.

Acid migration
Process that causes the acidity of one item to affect another.

Acrylic paint
Water-based, quick-drying synthetic paint. Can be dry brushed, texturized, thinned with water for color washes, or used to alter the color of page elements.

Adhesive
Products that affix photos, paper or embellishments to another surface. Types vary depending on the desired application. Varieties include adhesive dots, dimensional tape, double-stick tape, glue sticks, liquid glues, photo splits, sprays and tabs. Many are available in permanent and repositionable formats.

Aging
Method used to give cardstock, paper, embellishments and photos an antiqued or distressed appearance. Techniques include sanding, crumpling, inking, dry brushing and staining.

Album
Book used with page protectors to store completed layouts. Traditional styles include three-ring, strap-hinge, post and spiral bindings.

Altered
When the appearance of an item (anything from patterned paper to composition notebooks to CDs) is transformed with inks, paints, art media or ephemera.

Analogous colors
Shades located directly next to each other on a color wheel.

Appliqué
Hand-made or pre-made decorative accent. Can also refer to the process of producing layered, dimensional embellishments.

Archival
Products and materials proven to have a safe amount of acidic and buffered content.

Awl
Small tool with a tapered, pointed tip used to punch holes in leather and other materials.

b

Blender
Pencil or marker designed to soften, blend or seal chalked, water colored or stamped images.

Bone folder
Curved tool designed to help fold, crease, score and burnish cardstock.

Border
Decorative design used to adorn layout edges or accent peripheries.

Brad
Metal fasteners with prongs that can be inserted through multiple materials. Available in a variety of colors, sizes and finishes, these accents also work as decorative elements.

Brass template

Thin piece of brass with decorative cut-out shapes used for dry embossing and stenciling. See also *Embossing template*.

Brayer

Roller (available in different densities) used to spread ink and other media onto cardstock. Can also be used as a burnisher and to create resist and texture effects.

Buffered

Materials, such as paper, with a pH rating of 8.5 that contains a buffering agent to neutralize acidic contaminants.

Burnish

To rub material firmly (with a brayer, bone folder or other tool) to smooth, compact or set a fold or element.

Chalk

Available in a range of color palettes and applied with a sponge applicator, cotton ball, brush or fingertip, chalk can give a soft pastel color to backgrounds or images. Also ideal for shading and filling in stamped images.

Chalk ink

Dye and pigment inks that produce soft, powdery and often opaque images. Many varieties help stamped images stand out on dark-colored backgrounds.

Chipboard

Thick paper board used for a sturdy background, mini-album cover, shadow box frame, etc.

CK OK

Program designed to help scrapbookers identify archivally safe products. Products receive the "CK OK" seal of approval if they meet established preservation guidelines by preservation experts from *Creating Keepsakes*.

Clip art

Ready-made computer artwork that can be printed, cut and pasted to serve as accents or paper piecing patterns.

Collage

Combination of items—from memorabilia and mixed media to photos, clip art and stamped images—used to create a single decorative surface. Items are adhered and sealed with a glaze or decoupage medium.

Color blocking

Rectangular shapes of complementary or contrasting colors combined to produce striking backgrounds.

Color wash

Watered down watercolors, dyes or acrylic paints that can be applied to paper or accents to add subtle color.

Color wheel

Circular spectrum of colors designed to show shades that produce harmonious color schemes.

Complementary colors

Shades situated directly across from each other on a color wheel.

Concho

Metal fastener with several sharp prongs that are pushed through cardstock and bent flat to secure. Available in a variety of shapes, colors, sizes, designs and metals. Also referred to as "nailheads."

Corner rounder

Hand-held punch designed to remove sharp, 90-degree corners from photos, leaving curved, blunt edges.

Cropping

Trimming a photo (or other page element) to alter its composition or remove unnecessary or cluttered backgrounds. The act of scrapbooking is also referred to as "cropping."

Deacidification spray
Product designed to remove or neutralize the harmful qualities in acidic paper products.

Debossing
Dry-embossed image with the recessed side facing up instead of the raised side.

Decorative scissors
Cutting tools that produce a variety of decorative edges. Styles range from postage stamp edges and the torn deckle look to ornate flourishes and traditional pinking shear cuts.

Decoupage
Clear glaze used to adhere, seal and protect layers of memorabilia, illustrations or pictures layer by layer, resulting in a decorative collage.

Die cut
Shape and letters created with a press and die that features sharp steel rules to cut through cardstock or other materials.

Dimensional adhesive
Liquid glue or glaze that retains its raised surface and shape after it dries.

Dry brushing
Application of acrylic (or other) paint using a stiff-bristled, dry paint brush.

Dye ink
Water-based, quick-drying ink. Check package label for permanent, removable and acid-free qualities.

Embellishment
Any type of accent, decoration or adornment used to embellish or promote the theme of a layout.

Embossing gun
Hand-held electric tool that blows hot air on a concentrated spot to melt embossing powder or enamel. Can also be used to quickly dry stamped or printed ink.

Embossing ink
Clear or slightly tinted sticky ink designed to use with embossing powder because of its lengthy drying time. Chalk can also be applied over the ink to produce soft designs.

Embossing pen
Clear or colored embossing ink in a pen form. Available in a variety of tip shapes and sizes for easy application with words, hand-drawn designs and tight spots.

Embossing powder
Fine powder (in a rainbow of colors) designed to be sprinkled over embossing ink, then melted with an embossing gun for shiny, raised results.

Embossing template
Brass or plastic sheet featuring cut-out shapes. Used with a light box and stylus to create dry-embossed images. See also *Brass template*.

Encapsulation
Completely sealing off photos or memorabilia to prevent acid migration or damage from other items.

Ephemera
Items, such as tickets, postcards, labels and other dimensional images that can be used in collage and to adorn layouts.

Eyelet
Round or shaped metal fastener attached with an eyelet setter to flatten and secure. Also known as "grommets" or "rivets." See also *Eyelet setter*.

Eyelet setter
Metal tool with a cone- or star-shaped tip that must be pressed or hammered to flatten the back of an eyelet. See also *Eyelet*.

Fibers
Yarn or strings available in numerous colors, textures and thicknesses. Can be used to hang other accents, tie items together or simply add dimension.

Fixative
Spray that dries to a matte or glossy finish to seal and protect artwork from smearing or smudging.

Focal point
Element on a layout designed or positioned to immediately catch the viewer's eye.

Gel medium
Cloudy medium used to texturize, adhere, blend with paint or pigment powder or transfer images. Some varieties feature colors or inclusions, such as micro beads or sand.

Gel pen
Ball-point pen with smooth-flowing opaque or metallic ink. Lighter colors are easily visible on dark background.

Gesso
Water-based medium, often created from a mixture of whiting and glue, used to prime surfaces (such as canvas or metal) for painting or gilding.

Gilding
Coating the edges or surface of an item with a thin metallic finish.

Gold leaf flake
Tufts of lightweight flakes that can be applied to most surfaces with tacky liquid glue or double-stick tape for a metallic, textured finish. Also available in silver and other varieties.

Gum Arabic
Water-soluble gum (from the acacia tree) used as a binder for pigment powders or as a solution to increase the gloss of watercolors.

Half-pint
Album that typically holds 8½" x 5½" pages.

Heritage photos
Vintage, nostalgic photos that often document family, community or world history.

Hot foil pen
Battery-operated tool with a tip that heats up to transfer foil to backgrounds to create detailed metallic designs.

Hot glue
Solid glue sticks melted with an electric glue gun. Melted glue can be used as an adhesive or as the base for dimensional and textural effects.

Jewelry findings
Metal jewelry parts or components, such as hooks, clips and chains, which can be used to embellish scrapbook pages.

Journaling
Text on a layout, which often tells the story behind the event or emotions showcased in the layout's photos.

Jute
Strong string or thin rope, often manufactured from plant fibers.

Lamination
Item sandwiched between two pieces of transparent adhesive sheets. Often used to protect fragile documents and photos.

Layering
Overlapping items to create added dimension, texture or visual interest.

Light box
Electric or battery-operated light source used to illuminate template shapes during the dry embossing process.

Lightfast
Element that's resistant and colorfast to sunlight.

Lignin
Non-archival bonding chemical found in wood and wood-based materials that make it sturdy. When ground into a pulp, as with newspaper, the bonding agent weakens and the material becomes brittle and will yellow with age.

LSS
Abbreviation for "Local Scrapbook Store."

m

Masking
Covering an item (or a portion of it) to prevent it from being painted, chalked or inked as other sections are colored.

Matting
Mounting a material such as cardstock, patterned paper or fabric behind a photo or accent, with just a border showing around the periphery.

Memorabilia
Materials that document or commemorate past events, such as flyers, brochures, newspaper clippings, postcards and tickets.

Mesh
Woven paper or metal. Also metal or fabric screening and self-adhesive Magic Mesh.

Metallic rub-ons
Creamy medium that can be applied with a sponge, brush or fingertips to add metallic highlights to paper and accents.

Mica
Translucent, acid-free, heat-resistant "tiles" easily peeled into paper-thin layers for layering, pressing or heat embossing.

Mini-book
Small album that comes either ready-made or can be custom made with tags, cardstock and other elements. Can be attached to a layout, used as a theme book or presented as a gift.

Mixed media
Combining two or more art media (such as paint, collage or colored pencils) in a single piece of artwork.

Monochromatic
Color scheme using different shades of a single color.

Mosaic
Item comprised of numerous smaller pieces. Torn or cut cardstock may be combined to form a mosaic background, for example.

Mulberry paper
Thin, fibrous paper with rich colors that can be torn, layered or stamped. Produces a feathery edge when torn.

p

Paper crimper
Tool that uses two rollers to give a corrugated texture to cardstock, paper or metal sheets.

Paper piecing
Trimming, layering and gluing cardstock or other materials to re-create an image. Often based on a pattern, such as pictures from tole painting or coloring books.

Paper piercer
Metal tool with a needle-sharp point used to poke small holes.

Paper punch
Small tool constructed of metal and plastic that punches through cardstock, paper or metal to produce decorative shapes.

Paper trimmer
Tool designed to cut cardstock, paper or photos. Available in personal, guillotine or rotary styles. Some feature interchangeable blades that produce decorative edges and scoring marks.

pH factor
Number that reflects the acidity and alkalinity of paper.

Photo safe
Materials proven to be acid- and lignin-free, and safe to use on or near photographs.

Photo turn
Small, pointed metal piece attached with an eyelet or brad to secure photos or flat embellishments to a page.

Pick-up square
Hard rubber square that can "erase" excess dried adhesive.

Pigment ink
Slow-drying, fade resistant, permanent opaque ink. Ideal for heat embossing.

Pigment powder
Fine powder (often extracted from minerals) that can be combined with gum Arabic, paint, ink and other media to produce shimmery or textured finishes.

Pocket

Page element that holds memorabilia, journaling or additional photos on a page.

Polymer clay

Malleable clay that can be formed, stamped or impressed. Can be baked or air-dried to set, depending on the brands.

Post-bound album

Album featuring two or three short metal posts that screw together and hold top-loading page protectors. Most albums can be expanded with post extensions.

Printable canvas

Thin, sturdy material designed to run through inkjet printers without wrinkling or buckling.

Quilling

Narrow strips of paper coiled around a thin shaft, such as a quilling tool, toothpick or paper piercer. Tight swirls can be pinched, elongated or joined with others to created larger designs or motifs.

Quilting

Geometric shapes cut from cardstock or patterned paper and pieced together to form a larger image or background. Shapes can also be hand- or machine-stitched, then stuffed with batting or scrap paper for a raised appearance.

Red eye pen

Pen used to blot out red glare from a subject's eyes in photos.

Repositionable

Item secured with a non-permanent adhesive that can be removed and re-set numerous times.

Resist ink

Stamping ink that masks other inks. For example, when an image is stamped with resist ink and then covered with dye-based ink, the image will show through with a "ghosted" appearance.

Reverse stamping

Creating a faux bleached look by applying layers of ink to glossy cardstock or vellum, then pressing an un-inked stamp onto the surface to lift ink away.

Rub-ons

Alphabet and images that can be transferred to backgrounds with a burnisher. Note: Metallic rub-ons are also referred to as "rub-ons."

Sanding

Rubbing sandpaper, steel wool or a wire brush to distress and scrape away the top layer of patterned paper, white-core cardstock or pre-printed accents.

Scoring

Using a special blade or sharp object to emboss a line into cardstock to create a crisp fold.

Scraplift

Copying part or all of a page design, element or aspect of another scrapbooker's layout for your own creation.

Self-healing mat

Flexible cutting surface (ideal for use with craft knives, eyelet setters and some circle cutters) that doesn't show wear, even after multiple cuts.

Shadow box

Shallow "case" designed to protect an item. On layouts, a shadow box can be created with mat board and a transparency to inset dimensional accents.

Shaker

Sealed shadow box with loose accents, such as beads, confetti or punches beneath a clear window.

Sheet protector

Clear sleeve designed to hold a completed scrapbook page. Only acid- and polypropylene-free versions should be used for archival projects.

Shrink plastic

Plastic sheets that can be stamped, printed or written on, then trimmed and heated in the oven or with a heat gun. Heated images will shrink and thicken.

Side-loading
Page protectors that open along the sides and are designed to cover layouts. Created for use with strap-hinge and spiral-bound books.

Slide mount
Plastic or cardboard holder designed to frame a slide. Can be used as a mini-frame for small photos or embellishments.

Solvent ink
Opaque ink that dries quickly on most surfaces, including metal, glass, plastic and fabric. Requires a special cleaner to be completely removed from stamps.

Spiral bound
Album featuring pages bound with a metal coil. Pages must be used as layout backgrounds or covered with cardstock or patterned paper. Requires side-loading page protectors.

Split complementary colors
Colors situated on either side of a color's complementary shade on a color wheel. See also *Complementary colors.*

Sponging
Using a cosmetic, kitchen or sea sponge to apply stamping ink or art medium to cardstock or other materials.

Spritzer
Manually operated "air gun" that forces air across the tip of a marker, blowing the ink onto the paper in a concentrated spray.

Stamp
Rubber, acrylic, or foam shape that is dipped in ink or paint and is used to create an image on various materials.

Stamp positioner
Small "L"-shaped tool that assists in placing stamped images in specific places. Used with transparencies, tissue paper or a clear acrylic plate.

Stencil
Cardboard, plastic or metal piece featuring a cut out shape. Ink or paint can be brushed over the opening to transfer the image to another element. The stencil itself can also be decorated as an accent.

Stickers
Glossy or matte self-adhesive images, words and designs.

Stippling
Tapping a round brush into ink or paint and pouncing it onto paper or cardstock to produce a textured or mottled finish.

Stitching
Adorning a layout with machine or hand sewing. The process of joining two halves to form one 12" x 12" computer scan is also known as "stitching."

Strap-hinge
Album with pages (that must be used as the layout background or covered with other paper) held together with a plastic strap. Requires side-loading page protectors.

Stylus
Blunt, round-tipped tool designed to press into cardstock (or other materials) to produce dimensional images. Usually used with a shape template.

Swap
Exchange of supplies, ideas or completed projects between fellow scrapbookers.

T-square
Drafting tool with a long ruler and cross bar used to draw straight and parallel lines. Can also assist in making long, straight cuts.

Tags
Strips of paper that may have a hole at the top for looping string. Available in a variety of sizes, colors and themes. Cut from cardstock, vellum and fabric, they can be used as backgrounds for other embellishments, journaling and as photo mats or mini-book pages.

Template
Negative portion of a cut-out shape, usually made of brass, cardboard or plastic. Template shapes can be drawn and cut out or traced with an embossing stylus to create dimensional designs.

Three-ring

Album featuring three round or "D"-shaped rings that hold top-loading page protectors. Easy to add and remove pages, but with a wide gutter between facing pages.

Tiles

Shaped accents created from metal, cardboard or acrylic. They can be embellished with stamps, inks, paints and other media.

Top-loading

Page protectors that open along the top and are designed to cover layouts. Created for use with post-bound or three-ring albums.

Transparency

Heat-resistant clear acetate that can be used as an overlay, shaker window or background. Can serve as a slick surface for stamping or printing. Pre-printed styles are also available.

Vellum

Semi-translucent paper available in a variety of colors and textures for layering, stamping, dry embossing, texturing and more.

Walnut ink

Rich brown liquid (sometimes created from walnut shells), used to dye, stain or color wash paper, fabric and other materials. Available in liquid, ink and crystal forms.

Watercolor pencils

Colored pencils that can be turned into watercolors by mixing with water or a blender pen.

index

Are you looking for a scrapbook layout about a particular subject? Layout subjects are identified by the term "layout" following the subject. This index also provides a reference of tools and techniques featured in this book.

Creating Keepsakes is located at 14850 Pony Express Road, Bluffdale, UT
84065. Phone: 801/984-2070. Fax: 801/984-2080. Home page:
www.creatingkeepsakes.com

E-mail to the editorial offices may be sent to editorial@creatingkeepsakes.com

For subscription information on *Creating Keepsakes* magazine, call or write:
Phone: 386/447-6318
International: 386/445-4662
E-mail: creatingkeepsakes@palmcoastd.com

Subscriber Services
Creating Keepsakes
P.O. Box 420235
Palm Coast, FL 32142-0235